# THE
# REST
# OF OUR
# LIVES

## Also by Judy Goldman

MEMOIRS

*Child*

*Together: A Memoir of a Marriage
and a Medical Mishap*

*Losing My Sister*

NOVELS

*Early Leaving*

*The Slow Way Back*

POETRY

*Wanting to Know the End*

*Holding Back Winter*

# THE REST OF OUR LIVES

A Memoir

*Judy Goldman*

—BLAIR—

Printed in the United States of America
Cover design and painting by Laurie Smithwick
Interior design by April Leidig

Blair is an imprint of Carolina Wren Press.

*The mission of Blair/Carolina Wren Press is to seek out, nurture, and promote
literary work by new and underrepresented writers.*

We gratefully acknowledge the ongoing support of general operations by the Durham
Arts Council's United Arts Fund and the North Carolina Arts Council.

Library of Congress Control Number: 2024948426
ISBN: 978-1-95-888854-4

*For my grandchildren, Zoe, Lucy, Tess, and Ben.*
*The instant you were born,*
*you curled a finger around my heart.*

Old age is the most unexpected of all the things that happen to a man. —LEON TROTSKY

Old age is the most unexpected of all the things that happen to a woman. —JUDY GOLDMAN

We learn only in old age what happened to us in our youth. —GOETHE

# Prologue

S pring Break, six of us drove from Rock Hill to Ocean Drive, just south of Myrtle Beach. In South Carolina, you could get a driver's license at fourteen, so we'd had ours for a couple of years. We stayed at my friend's family's house, an old, barely standing house a few rows back from the ocean. It was wood, painted white but needed painting—actually, needed a lot more than just paint. The weather was unseasonably cold, and the house had no heat. But who needed heat in a beach house in the 1950s?

Usually, one or two mothers chaperoned, but none of ours could go this time, so we asked a woman who was a friend of one of our mothers. Maybe it was the cold. Maybe it was being with a houseful of teenaged girls; she had a son, a quiet son. Maybe she was an alcoholic, something nobody talked about then. But she stayed drunk all five days, barely venturing out of her bedroom, only wobbling out for instant coffee.

We did our own version of rule breaking. We smoked. Everyone but me. I just could not learn how to inhale. I tried, over and over. Smoking was glamorous; coughing was not. Still, I knew how to hold a cigarette, the same way my mother did—I had studied her and practiced in front of a mirror—right elbow resting in my left hand, my thumb against the two fingers curled under.

During the day, we lay on the beach in our bathing suits, towels decorated with seashells or fish spread beneath us, cardigans pulled tight around our skinny bodies, hair blowing in our eyes, stuck to our lashes. We were willing the temperature to rise.

Nights, we put on more make-up than we ever used at home, including mascara, and walked to The Pad, a bar as ramshackle as the house we were staying in—raw wood ceiling and cracked railings, open on all sides, the music of our youth blaring, rock 'n' roll records. We were there to meet boys. Standing side by side, spaced a little apart, we leaned against the railing, smoking (or just holding a cigarette), hoping a very cute boy from Gaffney or Spartanburg or Tabor City would ask us to dance. Not a good feeling to be the only one *not* asked to dance. Believe me, I know. Not a good feeling at all.

Another chilly April, years later, friends and I head to Litchfield Beach, just north of Ocean Drive, to my friend's lovely and warm oceanfront house. There are five of us, my Breakfast Group, friends since our children were teenagers, three of us still able to drive on the interstate, two not able: me because I can't see far-off signs and the other because she gets lost.

I left my husband at home with a list on the kitchen counter of things to do:

*1. Don't forget to take all three Gabapentins every day.*
*2. Physical therapist coming Monday at 11:30.*
*3. Keep your cell phone in your pocket, in case you fall.*
*4. Drink water.*

We do not get out to the beach, too cold, although we sit on the deck overlooking the ocean and drink wine before dinner. Dinner is healthy, boiled shrimp and corn on the cob one night, rotisserie chicken and salad the next. None of us wants to gain more weight.

One thing I feel I must add: When I took that long-ago beach trip, I packed my padded bra. For this more recent trip, I packed my heating pad, because I never know when my back might go out.

———

One story toppling into another. I'm always comparing what I think and do now to what I thought and did when I was young. This beach trip reminds me of that beach trip.

This tentative step is like that tentative step.

This knotty decision is like that knotty decision.

This loss is like that loss.

The details couldn't be more different—I get that—but today reminds me of yesterday because inside, I'm just a kid. Regardless of our age, we're all still kids, grappling. Trying to find the opening in our uncertainty. That feeling, back then, of not being ready for what came next is like this feeling, right now, of not being ready for what comes next.

Wait. I'm eighty. Shouldn't I have caught on by now how to *be ready*?

Oh, goodness, if ever there was a time of not being ready for the next thing, it's in old age. We all know what's next. Are we ever ready?

My way of preparing is to reassemble certain memories—genesis stories, I call them, stories that go to the heart of each life passage. Touchstones. That back-and-forthing. Where we are, where we've been, how time is a circle, the world repeating itself, endlessly. My life now, hinged to my life then.

At times, I even find myself comparing a genesis story of mine to someone else's genesis story—my older sister's, my mother's, my grandmother's. Another kind of back-and-forthing. As though families have themes running through them.

So, what am I trying to say in these pages?

That turning eighty is a lot like turning sixteen, thirty-five, sixty— how we keep entering uncharted territory, over and over?

That old age is really not so different from young age?

Maybe this: The past is just sitting in our palms.

# 1.

We were the type of family that had a genesis story for every significant stage we passed through on our way to the future, each portal. We were in love with beginnings. Endings, not so much. We didn't invent the idea of genesis stories; we probably just venerated them more than most people. I wish you could've seen my parents; my brother, Donald (eight years older); my sister, Brenda (three years older); and me around the Thanksgiving table—talking, talking, through the turkey and cornbread dressing and pineapple-ringed sweet potato casserole, all the way to ambrosia. Or in our two-toned green Oldsmobile, windows rolled down, engine softly humming, driving home to Rock Hill on a summer Sunday evening after a visit with Mother's sisters and their families in Columbia. Or under the fringed umbrella at the round wrought iron picnic table in our backyard, eating ham biscuits and deviled eggs, drinking sweet iced tea. All those times together we filled the space with our stories, told them over and over in great detail, the expression on our faces always a small *wow*.

Here's the first genesis story I ever heard—how my parents met, the very beginning of them:

It was 1929. My mother, Margaret Bogen, was twenty and living with her parents and working as a bookkeeper at South Carolina Power & Light in tiny Denmark (down the road from tiny Norway,

tiny Sweden, and tiny Finland in South Carolina's Low Country).
Jewish people in southern towns were always traveling to the closest
city to socialize with other Jewish people. This evening, my mother
was at a dance in Charleston, where she'd been named "Queen of the
Ball," and she was dancing with her date. I imagine her hand on his
neck, his hand on her back, the band playing something like "Always"
or "Bye, Bye, Blackbird," saxophone, clarinet, piano. I also imagine
her bobbed hair, strappy heels, short and flouncy dress, maybe purple velvet. Of course, there was her radiant, inviting beauty, her valentine face; you just did not want to look away from her.

Times were so hard (the Great Depression), my father had had to
drop out of his second year at Emory Law School to work in a family friend's shoe store in Newberry, South Carolina, the only job he
could find. He arrived at the dance late, with a carful of buddies, all
of them drunk, some falling-down drunk, though not my father,
who was merely drunk. Ben Kurtz would never be falling-down anything. He had too much dignity. He was upright in every way. Pos-
ture *and* morals. High forehead, tall and lean, nice-looking. But the
story goes, he and his buddies—jackets awry, ties loose—tumbled
into the banquet hall, called way too much attention to themselves
with their boisterous talking and laughing, hid their liquor bottles under a table—a deed even more rogue at the time because of
Prohibition.

The minute my father saw Mother and her date dancing, he cut
in. She scanned the room looking for a way out, and with a sneer
that's hard for me to imagine yet so much a part of the story, she said
to him, "You're just the type I hate—late to the party, drunk, bottle
under the table . . ."

He replied, a sneer on *his* face, easier to imagine, not because he was a sneering person, but because he could be prickly, "And you're just the type I hate—everybody's sweetheart, queen of the dance, Miss Beauty Queen..."

I don't know how long they kept on dancing and insulting each other. I know they didn't even introduce themselves, did not tell their names. Maybe one of them walked away in the middle of the song. Maybe the song was over, and my mother went back to her date and my father went back to whatever he went back to. However their encounter ended, it ended. That was it for the two of them.

Two years later, a mutual friend who knew nothing of their history fixed them up on a blind date. That night, on that blind date, in those new circumstances, my mother and father fell instantly in love.

I've always been enthralled with the story for two reasons:

One, I bask in the glory of having a beautiful mother. I would never have been queen of any dance. Never would have been Miss Denmark or runner-up to Miss South Carolina, as she was. Maybe that's why I love telling this story. I learned of the beauty contests when I took apart an old, framed photo of Mother and found the newspaper article folded inside. After Mother died, her older sister, Emma, told me that when Mother was first asked to enter the Miss Denmark contest, she told the contest chairman to ask Emma instead. Mother wore her beauty the way I might wear a soft, comfortable corduroy shirt—she really didn't seem to think about it at all. Beauty is not what I'm known for, but because my mother was known for her beauty, I can float on the periphery of what she showed the world.

Here's the second reason I love the story: It's the only time I've ever heard of my father getting drunk. I never saw him bring a glass of beer, wine, or bourbon to his lips. It's not that he was against drinking or gave it up because he drank too much. It's that he suffered from cluster headaches, and any type of alcohol could bring them on. So, he just did not drink. You can see why the night he met Mother, the night he was so drunk, shocks me. To picture him drunk, to picture him even a little boisterous, to picture him hiding a bottle under a table is to conjure an image that is so *not* him; it's as if I'm watching that earnest, pensive man let loose on the accordion.

One more thing about the story that gets me: how hate so seamlessly turned to love. Can you even trust a love that happens in an instant? I know it's easy to dismiss the idea of love at first sight. Many people think it's a foolish, fairy-tale notion. I'm not one of those people. I believe love is mysterious. Miraculous. Of course, love at first sight requires a measure of innocence. And hope. Still, I think it's possible to feel an immediate and overpowering connection to another person. My family believes in love at first sight. It happens to us over and over, generation after generation.

My grandparents (my mother's parents) were first cousins but had never met. When they each immigrated to New York City from Poland or Russia (depending on which year you're looking at the border), they ended up renting rooms down the hall from each other in a relative's boarding house on the Lower East Side. They fell instantly in love. The family was horrified! *First cousins cannot get married!* But love overruled what some states in this country still outlaw.

A couple of generations later, my sister met her husband on a New Year's Eve blind date. They were college sophomores. When she called home on January 1, my parents and I were on three different phones, listening to her gush over a "real tall, real good-looking, real nice" guy. I wrote down everything she said because I knew she'd just met the person she would marry. (I was just a teenager but could recognize a good genesis story.) By spring, they were engaged. At their rehearsal dinner, the night before their December wedding, I used my dashed-off notes as my toast.

With my parents, it was an immediate and overpowering aversion, then an immediate and overpowering attraction. But the attraction was lasting. For years they sat knee to knee on our red leather sofa, watching *I Love Lucy*, their hands clamped together. My father's birthday and anniversary cards to Mother were so big and elaborate they came in thin 8" x 10" cardboard boxes. His standard signature: *Your Bennie always.*

# 2.

You don't question genesis stories. They're their own category. They're built on exaggeration, chance, synchronicity, emotion, and irony. They're romantic. They're promise-heavy. They live outside the realm of exactness. And they make life seem less random, less like the events of our lives have just been tossed at us haphazardly. We can almost see a divine plan in place. Of course, we can't detect any pattern when we're living a genesis story. It's only in the recall that we think of the word *bashert*, Yiddish for "meant to be, fated, inevitable." We reach across time and connect the dots between genesis stories. Yoke the stories together, even though the events they chronicle happen decades apart.

Like my parents, like my grandparents, like my sister and brother-in-law, my husband and I have a genesis story that pivots on passion and feels like a small miracle. Because all my life I'd heard the stories of my parents' and grandparents' romances and I'd witnessed my sister's, I expected a *pow* of my own. I've always known that when something *feels* extraordinarily right, it probably *is* extraordinarily right.

I've written about the beginning of Henry and me before, in essays, in other books. But, of course, that's what you do with these stories. Repeat, repeat. Here it is again, with a few details I haven't told before:

After graduating from the University of Georgia, after teaching high school English in Atlanta for two years, I was living in New York City. I had just quit my secretarial job and was about to begin my dream job, copywriter for an advertising agency. Between jobs, I flew home to Rock Hill to visit my parents. My sister Brenda and Henry's sister Ruth knew each other and wanted to fix Henry and me up on a blind date. I was not thrilled to be fixed up. I hadn't brought "dating clothes" with me, and really, all I'd wanted was to spend time with my parents. Plus, I'd started dating someone in New York. I found out later Henry was just as unthrilled. He told his sister, "Now that I live in the same town as you, you're going to be tempted to introduce me to girls. Don't! I can get my own dates!"

Neither of us said no.

This is where our meeting starts to feel fated, *bashert*.

Days before my trip home, my New York roommate and I had been guests of her aunt and uncle at the Copacabana, where Diana Ross and the Supremes were appearing. We had ringside seats in that glittery room. After dinner and before the show, a fortune teller made her way from one small round table to the next. She was all shiny gold, blousy, red-painted lips, silk headscarf. My roommate's aunt motioned her over. She pulled up a chair and nodded at me, so I held out my hand, palm up on the table. Neither of us needed to say a word. *Preprogrammed* isn't a romantic enough word for her nod and my reach across the table, but that's how it felt—as though the two of us were already in cahoots about my future. She moved her forefinger in a slow graze over the creases in my hand. I'd never really paid attention to those creases before. Now I was wondering what they were saying. Then, as if she knew the impact of a dramatic pause, she got stone-still and just stared at my palm. I worried maybe she'd seen something so tragic she didn't know whether to reveal it or not. Maybe I even held my breath for a second. But she looked up and smiled, those red, red lips, and said, "You will soon meet a tall, handsome redhead."

My blind date, Henry, had grown up in the Bronx and Miami Beach, graduated from the University of Florida and then optometry school in Chicago. He had just moved to Charlotte (twenty-eight miles from Rock Hill) to go into practice with another doctor. Months into that job, he quit to open his own office. That's when we met. I was twenty-five. He was twenty-seven.

I hadn't been picked up for a date at my parents' house since high school. What was even more awkward—Mother was hosting her music club that night. I sure didn't want to bring a blind date into a living room filled with the Allegro Music Club. I told Henry to drive to Rock Hill, stop at the first gas station he came to, and call. I'd meet him there.

Brenda and her husband, Chuck, lived in Rock Hill at the time, so they dropped me off at the Pure Oil station at the corner of Cherry Road and Oakland Avenue. Henry was parked next to a pay phone, across from the gas pumps, waiting for me. I slipped out of Brenda and Chuck's car, walked across the asphalt, got into Henry's Volkswagen Beetle, and we took off. We were both probably thinking, *Let's get this over with.*

Eyes on the road, he barely had a chance to look at me, but I got a good look at him.

Tall, handsome redhead.

Eyebrows, thick and dark. Big bull neck and shoulders. He wore a blue, short-sleeved, oxford-cloth shirt that had obviously been washed and pressed at the dry cleaner. Very neat appearance. Meticulous. His arms were furry, golden.

I'd already decided we'd go to the Holiday Inn coffee shop out on the bypass. Rock Hill was not exactly brimming with night spots. Our choice was either the Holiday Inn or the Elks Club, where my parents and their friends went for prime rib.

Inside the coffee shop, every square table was set, plates and glasses, silverware and white cloth napkins, as though any minute there'd be a rush of customers. But we were the only ones there. We ordered coffee and talked. There was a sunny goodness about this guy. And a confidence. He was smart and funny. He not only made me laugh; he laughed at the things I said. And he listened, really listened. And asked questions. If I'd had a list, every little box would've been checked. Our waitress filled. And refilled. Around eleven, the manager ambled over and drawled, "Listen here, folks, I'm closing up, but I'll leave a pot of coffee on, and you can just turn it off when you leave. Close the door behind you. It'll lock by itself."

We stayed till light was rising in the windows.

I don't think we remembered to turn off the coffee pot when we left.

Standing just inside the back door of my parents' house, in the laundry room, beside the washer and dryer, a basket of towels waiting to be washed, we were slowing down with our talking and moving toward saying good night. I knew what I had to do. I reached up and kissed him good night.

The next day, before I left for New York, I told my parents and sister that Henry was the one. I found out later he told his sister the same thing about me.

Three weeks passed, and I flew back to the Carolinas to see him.

Friday night we double-dated with Brenda and Chuck to the Pineville Dinner Theater, between Rock Hill and Charlotte. The two of us were so shining-eyed over each other, we hardly noticed that the rustic barn theater was fake rustic, the show was corny, and the steaks were tough.

Saturday afternoon, I borrowed bikes from my parents' neighbors, and Henry and I rode out into the country, picnicked on bread and cheese on a blanket in a grassy meadow, talked, made out. Saturday night we saw *Two for the Road*, starring Audrey Hepburn and Albert Finney, a movie that traces the arc of a marriage. I was already imagining our arc.

Then, a month of letters back and forth.

Then, he drove his Beetle to New York for the weekend.

I was nervous about his visit. *How do I make a great impression on this man I plan to marry? I should cook for him!* But I was not a very good cook. My repertoire was mainly French toast and tuna noodle casserole.

I bought Craig Claiborne's *The New York Times Cookbook* and decided to make what I thought was the most sophisticated recipe in the book—beef stroganoff. I needed to do a trial run first. A week before Henry's visit, I took the afternoon off from work and shopped and cooked. I invited Donald and his girlfriend, Wendy, who was editor of a food magazine (of all things!), for dinner that night.

The three of us sat at my kitchen table, the meat and onions and butter and sour cream swimming in our plates, not exactly coagulating, but starting to.

The room was quieter than I'd expected.

Wendy, usually eager to score points with my brother by being nice to me, was not saying a word. Neither was Donald. Surely, the compliments would start soon. They just needed to chew and swallow a few more times. But they were mostly just moving the food around on their plates with their forks.

Finally, Donald spoke up: "You better be good in bed!"

He reached into his pocket for his wallet and said, "Here. Take my American Express card. You and Henry go out to dinner!"

————

Henry stayed with his cousin on the West Side. I lived in a one-bedroom apartment on the East Side with a roommate. My memory is that Henry and I did not sleep together until our wedding night. Maybe I'd reverted to my 1950s-small-town-South way of thinking and doing, as though I had not broadened my horizons at all in New York, at least where love and lust were concerned (more on that later). Maybe, because this was only our third date, I didn't think we knew each other well enough. (What's funny is that we got married so fast, we really didn't know each other well enough *after* our wedding.) Henry's memory is that we had sex once before we were married, later that summer, and then decided to wait. Which one of us is right, we have no idea. We've been wrangling over this for fifty-four years.

Here's the most important thing about the Friday night after he arrived in New York: We said the words *I love you*. He said them first; I blissfully followed.

Saturday night, we went out for Italian food in the neighborhood. (I did not use Donald's credit card; Henry took care of the check.) After dinner, we walked arm in arm back to my apartment, lay side by side on the sofa I'd found abandoned on the curb, the cushions oddly stuffed with sawdust (a little always sifted out when you sat down). We talked, we kissed, we talked. Our conversation was smooth and lazy—when would we see each other again, where would we go from here. It was a conversation that had the future stamped all over it.

I asked what I thought was the logical next question: "Can you picture us growing old together?"

No answer.

I gathered my breath, let it out, tried to think. Had I just ruined everything? Had our relationship ground to a halt? Can you even call a third date a relationship?

He still wasn't saying a word. Was there any way to reel back my question?

Finally, in a deep-throated voice, he said, "Hmm. That's a loaded question."

Loaded question? We had a lot to talk about.

He said he couldn't afford to get married. He'd just signed a lease for his new office.

I said I'd be able to get a good job in Charlotte, having worked at a New York ad agency.

He said there was the mammoth loan he'd applied for. He had exactly ninety dollars in his checking account.

I said whatever I needed to say to offset that.

The same way I would talk myself into a job, I was talking him into marrying me. I kept at it until daybreak. Until we got engaged.

———

What I find interesting about the question I asked, which nearly derailed everything, is that I was thinking about old-age romance when I was so young. But then, I've always been fascinated by the stages in a life. Even when I was going full blast, I imagined what it would be like when my pace slackened with age and time started to run out. When I was in my forties or fifties—young!—I Scotch-taped a poem to my desk that expressed how endearing it is to see old men kindly carry their wives' pocketbooks. Maybe I've always thought that old age is just a fairy tale, a time in our lives when a bad fairy puts a curse on us. But wait—all is not lost. Love—a kiss—can save us.

———

Picture Henry in his navy swim trunks, me in my green-and-white-flowered bikini. We're holding hands, circling the pool on our way out to the ocean, spending five days in Puerto Rico on our honey-moon, a honeymoon we can't afford. We had decided to skip the honeymoon. But, in a private conversation, my father asked me if Henry and I planned to go on a honeymoon. When I told him no, too expensive, he said he really thought we should plan one, that a hon-eymoon is a special time, important for a young couple starting out, go, have fun, take a vacation together! He reminded me that he and Mother had splurged on a weekend in Atlanta after their wedding in Columbia, even though it was the heart of the Great Depression and the banks had closed the day before they got married and they'd lost just about everything. My father's insistence on a honeymoon was, in one way, surprising. He was practical, matter-of-fact, frugal. I once wrote a poem about him with the title "No Foolishness About Him." In another way, his stance was not surprising. There was a bit of the romantic in him. Maybe I had sensed that side of him all the years I'd heard him shaving at the bathroom sink, singing "Ah, Sweet Mystery of Life."

Coincidentally, Henry's dad had the same private conversation with him, encouraging him not to skip the honeymoon. Another romantic. My father-in-law owned a cafeteria that served breakfast, lunch, and dinner, so he left for work at sunrise. He used to leave love notes on his pillow for Henry's mom to find when she woke up.

When Henry and I revealed these conversations to each other, he asked, "Did your dad offer to help pay for a honeymoon?"

I answered, "Well, no. Did yours?"

"Well, no."

So, here we are, "Ode to Billy Joe," the popular song this August 1967, on loudspeaker in the pool area, the two of us stepping carefully around the lounge chairs circling the pool, on our way to our private spot on the beach, the silky sand, rippled water, those romantic fathers of ours back home satisfied after talking us into a honeymoon, the sunshiny days my new husband and I are spending just with each other, our skin glowing with sweat and youth.

# 3.

My parents had been married a few months and were living in Newberry, when my father, driving to visit his brother in Charlotte, passed through Rock Hill. It was 1932. My father was immediately attracted to Rock Hill's two-lane, block-long Main Street with its handful of shops, the shingle-roofed Southern Railway depot at the end of Main Street, the charming women's college and sculpted stone fountain at its center, cotton fields and textile mills, hints of the good life those young people—Mother, twenty-two; Daddy, twenty-three—were dreaming of.

They rented a small house on Confederate Avenue. (Confederate Avenue. Now that's a genesis story all to itself! Small town, deep South, tarnished history. The street still exists, even today.) My father borrowed money from the owner of the shoe store in Newberry and opened The Smart Shop, a women's clothing store, on Main Street, between Good Drug Store and Belk. He also opened King's Men's Shop a few doors down.

With the birth of my brother, Donald, a year later, my parents outgrew their rental house and set their sights on living in the Cherry Park area of town, close to the college, a neighborhood of dogwood trees and azaleas, sidewalks, the scent of cut grass, tomatoes ripening on windowsills.

842 Eden Terrace was for sale. A white clapboard, two-story house with gray shutters and a small paved patio out front. Woods next door. Front yard so shady there was, of course, a concrete bench under the largest oak. The second largest oak was begging Mother to plant a little garden around it, fill it with red tulips in the spring, red geraniums in the summer.

My parents called Uncle Irwin, my mother's sister's husband, who was in the construction business in Columbia. He could tell them if this would be a smart purchase. He'd know if the house was well constructed, had any problems that would tell them to keep looking.

He strolled through the rooms with that wonderful, knowing look on his face, moved chairs and lifted the corners of rugs to inspect floors and baseboards, crept down the rickety steps to the basement, crawled up the pull-down stairs to the attic, assessed the exterior, the foundation.

"Keep looking," he said. "It's not well built. The floor plan is terrible. Definitely do not buy this house."

They bought it.

And they lived in that poorly constructed, poorly planned, large-hearted house for thirty-one years. Even though the basement flooded when it rained, even though my parents had to cut through my sister's and my bedroom to get to theirs, even though the door in the breakfast room that led to the side yard was permanently stuck, even though the washing machine was located in the minuscule downstairs guest bathroom and the dryer rumbled in the equally minuscule screened porch out back. We lived at 842 Eden Terrace until 1964, when I was living on my own after college.

We'd almost moved in 1955, when I started high school. My parents had bought a lot just outside the city limits and were ready to build. But because I did not want to live so far from my school and my friends, because I was the baby of the family, because I was spoiled and if I were unhappy, Mother did whatever she needed to do to fix that, my parents sold the lot.

Nine years later, in 1964, after I'd graduated from college and had been teaching in Atlanta for a year—It's safe! Judy's gone for good!—they bought a different lot in the same neighborhood and built a brick ranch overlooking the thirteenth hole of the golf course. I never really felt connected to the new house, but it brought my parents great joy. They were tired of living in an old house, tired of the bedroom arrangement, the wet basement, stuck door, hard-to-get-to washer and dryer. They wanted new. Every night after dinner, my father crossed the backyard and hit balls down the thirteenth fairway until he lost track of them in the fading light.

———

Visualizing the rooms of the house on Eden Terrace is what often leads me into sleep at night. Thoughts of the rooms of my childhood fill me with comfort and balance.

The knotty pine den and the floor-to-ceiling walls of books, all those serious spines, dark red, brown, black. Our family photos framed in bamboo above the fireplace, close to a hundred sweeping across— my favorite, a snapshot of twelve-year-old Donald at camp holding high the tail end of a dead rattlesnake, the same length as my brother was tall. Holding a snake in his bare hands, even a dead snake, in my mind was presidential-award-level bravery.

My small desk occupied one corner, my sister's slightly larger desk the other, bulletin boards hanging above them. I was too young to know what to do with a bulletin board, so when I saw my sister thumbtacking all kinds of things to hers, I clipped a cartoon from *The Saturday Evening Post* and thumbtacked it to mine: Two women wearing hats, one says to the other, "Whenever I'm down in the dumps, I buy a new hat." The other replies, "Oh, so that's where you get them." I had no idea what a dump was or what the cartoon meant. I was just happy my bulletin board was no longer blank cork.

Lining the double windowsill along the back wall of the den was a row of African violets, deep purple or really deep purple, depending on how the sunlight shifted.

There were built-in painted cupboards in the breakfast room, one holding flowery cotton tablecloths and napkins, the other our dishes.

Into the night, I reconstruct in my mind every inch of that house: the landing at the top of the stairs and the cedar chest holding sweaters in summer, bathing suits and summer pajamas in winter—where you sat when you talked on the big, black, rotary phone attached to the wall, the spiral cord you twirled around your fingers.

And let's not forget the faceted glass doorknobs; the wallpaper with floaty red-and-blue bachelor's button flowers in the bedroom my sister and I shared; the attic fan and the crisp, almost spicy scent of the breeze it stirred up, which I could identify even now.

# 4.

What will be the genesis story of my husband's and my next place? The *next place* is what preoccupies most everyone I know my age. Where will we feel more ready for what lies ahead? Where should we be living, fully deposited in this last narrow section of our lives?

Henry and I started married life in 1967 with my move into his one-bedroom bachelor apartment on Abbey Place in Charlotte, which he'd furnished with Aaron Rents furniture. The basics: double bed, bureau, sofa, end table, lamp, kitchen table, and two chairs. The apartment building looked like an old-time motel: a parking lot led to the skinny iron stairway, which led up to the open catwalk and the line of front doors so flimsy you could probably have kicked them in with little effort.

In 1969, when I was pregnant with our daughter, Laurie, we began our search for a bigger place. Should we rent another apartment? Stretch and buy a house? Evenings, Henry and I, both deliberate and careful with our money, sat at our pretend-wood kitchen table and added columns of numbers. Okay, not ready to buy. We looked at apartments, not many in Charlotte then.

One day I drove by a red brick duplex with a narrow wooden flower box the entire length of the front porch at the corner of Wonderwood Drive and busy Randolph Road—a FOR RENT sign in the front yard. When I glanced in my rearview mirror, I spotted the rope hammock in the backyard, shaded by overhanging oak branches. I did a quick U-turn and knocked on the door.

The next day, I took Henry to see it. The owners, who lived in the other side, seemed very nice. And it was such a sweet place. Three bedrooms, one I could use as my office, since, after the baby arrived, I would leave my copywriting job at Kincaid Advertising and start freelancing. But the rent was more than we'd planned for. We went home to add new columns of numbers.

A few days later, we called the duplex owners to say we'd take it. But they had already rented it. We went back to looking for an apartment. Came close to taking one that was okay, nothing special. Mainly, affordable and available.

Then, a call saying the deal had fallen through and the duplex was ours. We filled a U-Haul with boxes and moved the following week.

I planted red plastic geraniums in the flower box because I had no idea how to do dirt, real flowers, fertilizer. There was a firepit in the backyard where the fun-loving husband/landlord invited his buddies to spend one full night every August roasting a whole pig. They drank beer and told stories and laughed from sunset to sunrise, his use of our section of the backyard for their annual picnic written into our rental contract. The wife was a nurse, a kindhearted nurse, who rushed over to our side of the duplex when our new baby rolled off the changing table and I picked her up and her head flopped, which made me think she'd broken her neck (she hadn't) and again when our baby had a rash and I thought she had an exotic disease (she didn't). Every new mother should have a nurse next door.

———

Then we bought a nondescript, interchangeable split-level in a neighborhood of nondescript, interchangeable split-levels (before mid-century houses became desirable). I never liked that house. I started reading FOR SALE ads in the newspaper the day after we moved in. But I'd thought we should buy it because it was spring 1972 and our son, Mike, was about to be born and we'd soon be a family of four, and Brenda and her husband, Chuck, and their four sons lived in a split-level close by. Even though my sister and I were different in many ways, I was in the habit of following her lead. *Isn't this the time you're supposed to move into a split-level?* We lived in that house for ten years. The one good thing: The neighborhood was like a child's drawing of a neighborhood—bikes left on their sides in front yards, children jumping on the trampoline next door, a cul-de-sac behind our house where the neighborhood kids played till they were called in for supper.

―――――

1981: Henry, forty-two, and I, forty, were on totally opposite sides when it came to deciding where we should live next. He wanted to buy a lot and build a contemporary house. I wanted an old bungalow in an old neighborhood. The same conversation over and over—"old is charming" or "new is fresh"—words we voiced so often they were like lyrics to a song.

"I think I've found a compromise house for you and Henry," our realtor said as she drove through the old neighborhood lined with sidewalks upended by the ropy roots of giant pin oaks. I was perking up. But then, she turned onto a newish street, no sidewalks, newly planted Bradford pear trees. She stopped at a red brick, one-and-a-half-story house—a *new* red brick, one-and-a-half-story house. So new, in fact, it wasn't even finished. The railing on the front porch had not been painted. Raw wood. Wood dormers, also unpainted. Scattered across the front yard (not yet a lawn): extension ladders, paint cans, heavy tools, workmen's jackets, a pair of sawhorses with a plank across.

"No," I said, looking at the yard, the house, then her, then twisting around to look at twelve-year-old Laurie in the back seat. She was probably sipping a Capri-Sun, her standard after-school snack, which I thought was healthy because it had an illustration of an orange on the package. If she and I liked a house, we took Henry and nine-year-old Mike to see it. We'd been doing this for almost a year.

I turned back to the realtor. "I don't think we need to go in. It *is* a beautiful old neighborhood, but the street is new. We can just skip seeing this house."

"Oh, Judy, I understand," the realtor said, dropping her car key in her purse and opening her door, "but we have an appointment, so we need to at least look at it. Let's just go in. We don't have to stay long."

The house was a classic Williamsburg style. The roof was thick, chunky slate; I later learned it was one-hundred-year-old slate brought over from a long-abandoned church. Because of the traditional architecture and slate roof, if you squinted you could almost pretend it was an old house.

"Okay," I said, "let's go in."

The house had been built by a couple who'd gotten caught during the recession not being able to cover construction costs. We were in a position to buy because Henry's parents and my parents had died and left us money. But who buys a partially built house? It had been on the market for quite a while, probably because of the unusual circumstances. Uncle Irwin would have said, "Are you crazy? Forget it!"

Inside the front door, in spite of thick cables and the high whine of men sawing, I could see the handcrafted woodwork—the generous molding and fireplaces and built-in bookcases in the den and living room, not stained or painted yet, but gracefully carved. Light trapped flecks of construction dust in every room, *and* there was a lot of light everywhere. The den was large and airy, the eat-in kitchen also large and airy. The living room off the primary bedroom was tiny, snug, just the right size for Henry and me to listen to our records when Laurie or Mike would have friends over in the den—I was beginning to picture it. The house felt casual. No formal rooms. Just right for the way our family lived. We could be happy in these rooms. Here's where the sofa would go, the framed bamboo photos I'd grown up with. Our wicker loveseat and rocker would be great on the screened porch. I outlined in my mind a garden to the right of the porch, the spot in bright sun. We'd be able to see spirea, peonies, black-eyed Susans, and phlox through the wide window in the primary bedroom.

Up the stairs—careful not to touch painted walls that still looked and smelled wet. One of the bedrooms had a window seat. Laurie immediately made herself comfortable leaning into the window, her shoulders rounded to hide what she was doing. But I could see that she was scribbling on a scrap of paper.

Then she slyly slipped me her note: *Buy this house!*

We bought it.

As for who finished the house, the contractor the original owner had hired did the work, only now we made the final decisions, though we had to make those decisions on the contractor's timetable.

*You need to pick kitchen countertops by noon today, or we'll install the red Formica the previous owner chose.*

*We're ready to stain the floors. Decide on a stain. Now.*

All that was pretty stressful. The contractor was in a great hurry to finish the job and get paid by the original owner. The original owner was in a great hurry to get paid by us. We were *not* in a hurry; we wanted time to make decisions. But when the house was finally finished, we felt as though we'd bought an old bungalow and renovated; we felt as though we'd bought a vacant lot and built new; it was easy for Henry and me both to feel we'd landed in our dream house.

We lived at 1121 Scotland Avenue for thirty-three years. It became our family's 842 Eden Terrace—the house our children would grow up in, the house we all would look back on with misty nostalgia, the house we'd tell stories about, the house we'd go out of our way to drive by. Those rooms—the upstairs landing where Laurie and Mike played Atari, Mike's bedroom and the dartboard and the holes in the wall where he missed (was he blindfolded when he threw the darts?), the under-the-dormer space where Mike plugged in a lamp and drew maps with his neighborhood buddy, the under-the-dormer space in Laurie's room where she stored her Coke cans from all over the world and everything else she collected—those rooms Laurie and Mike will conjure in their minds, just before sleep, in their old age.

End of summer, 2014, we sold the house to a young couple expecting their first child. Late afternoon, the day before the closing, Mike was out of town, but Henry, Laurie, and I each, independently, showed up inside, strolling through the rooms one last time. We gravitated to the upstairs landing where we sat on the floor way into the night, tearfully summoning moments spent within those walls.

A house itself can be a genesis story.

We'd lived on Scotland Avenue until Henry and I, ages seventy-five and seventy-three, bought a condo so close by we could've carried our mattress over on our backs. A fourth-floor, two-bedroom condo that everyone said was overpriced. Sell low, buy high—our financial strategy! If Uncle Irwin had still been alive, he would have been shaking his head, *no, no, no*. (Oh, Uncle Irwin, would anyone in our family ever make a smart home purchase?) We bought our overpriced condo from a couple who owned a stylish home furnishings store, so everything they'd left (curtains, bathroom mirrors, bedroom wallpaper, even the green paint on the living room walls) was tasteful. All we did was move in; we did not change a thing. I fell in love with the relaxed, open feel of the space, including the room where I write, the walls I covered with photographs (many of the bamboo-framed photos that had hung in the den on Eden Terrace, then up the stairwell on Scotland Avenue), a room barely big enough for my old rolltop desk (the last gift my father gave me). Henry and I both fell in love with the row of French doors in the living room and dining room that let in every bit of sunlight there is—so much natural light that I never hung curtains or blinds. Our view: treetops and blue. And the terrace, where many nights we sit side by side on the glider, its squeaks barely audible. We look at the stars and the flickering lights of planes leaving the airport and cruising in. One night, I coaxed our granddaughter Zoe, eleven years old then, to sit with me and watch the planes. She sat there, patient for maybe three minutes, then said, "No offense, Gaygay, but this is the sort of thing old people like to do."

I was so in love with our condo, I joked with Henry I hoped one day we would just drop dead on the living room floor. That's how long we would stay.

# 5.

But in 2021, seven and a half years after moving in, the question was back: Where should we live?

Stay here, in the condo?

Stay here and face the coming health challenges, however we can face them? Stay here and face the morning of our deaths? A stroke, heart attack, dementia, cancer, a fall and fractured hip? *Something's going to get us.*

Right now, Henry and I are among the oldest residents in the building. Do our neighbors wish we would leave? Do they fear having to look out for us, check on us when the elevator stops running or the power goes out? We've already had several fire scares and, since it would take Henry, who walks haltingly with a cane, a long, long time to walk down four flights of stairs, I left him upstairs while I rushed down to see if it was a real fire and I should alert a fireman that my husband is stuck up on the fourth floor and please go get him. When the fire alarm went off in the middle of the night, I left him half asleep in our bed. All the residents had emptied out of the building and were standing around the front yard, huddling in bathrobes and raincoats pulled modestly over pajamas and nightgowns. A neighbor asked me where Henry was. I told him I'd left him upstairs. "Judy," he joked, "I'm reporting you to Social Services!"

Henry and I have now checked out retirement communities in Charlotte and are considering moving to the one that's closest to where Laurie and her family and Mike and his live, to make looking out for us easier. Sharon Towers is a gracious brick multistory retirement community built in the early '60s, near one of the city's largest shopping centers, a retirement community that calls itself a "lifetime community." Henry and I have visited four times, met with the young and friendly saleswoman, taken the tour—indoor pool, exercise room, library, multiple restaurants. We've even looked at an available apartment, decided we should move, then decided we should stay put. Looked at a second apartment, decided we should move. Then, how can we possibly go there? Not ready.

Not ready to make this decision.

We never expected, when we got old, that we would need to figure out where to live. Did not know that deciding where we should live at eighty and eighty-two is just as perplexing as deciding where to live when we were expecting our first child. What turns into the place that turns into a genesis story? For a soon-to-be family of three—apartment or duplex? For a family of four—split-level or old bungalow or half-built Williamsburg? Condo or retirement community for two old people?

Is a retirement community a good thing or a bad thing?

It's a good thing because, if I don't feel like cooking, we can just take the elevator down for dinner. Since Henry no longer drives and we're too old to figure out DoorDash, it's up to me on a cold, dark, wintry night to drive across town to pick up mu shu chicken or hamburgers. Mike said his vision for us at Sharon Towers is my calling to tell him, "Last night I had the best dinner! A grilled cheese sandwich and tomato soup! I just went down, ordered, and there it was!"

Laurie's vision of us at Sharon Towers: "Mom, I imagine you and Dad having dinner with other couples downstairs. You get tired of conversation, like you always do, and you excuse yourself to go back up to your place. Dad, who never gets tired of conversation and is never ready to leave any social gathering, stays."

It's good because if we have a health emergency, we can get help immediately. A security guard is available every minute of every day. Medical directives and contact numbers for next of kin are stored in a special container in your refrigerator, so no matter who answers your call for help, they know where to find the info. Pretty ingenious, I'd say, since everyone has a refrigerator. "Lifetime communities" are good at streamlining problems and solutions.

Good, because everyone says you should move while you're still healthy, that you shouldn't wait until you *have* to move. My friend, Dannye, says, "We should go while we're still cute."

Good, because as we age, we lose friends. I have lost three close friends to cancer. Two others have moved to be closer to children and grandchildren. Sharon Towers would mean I'd make new friends.

Good, because Henry's life is circumscribed right now. Fifteen years ago, he had an epidural, a medical procedure so routine it's given to women in childbirth. We had hoped the injection would relieve his back pain. But something went terribly wrong, and he was instantly paralyzed from the waist down. Over the coming weeks, his left leg came back, though spotty. His right leg remains paralyzed. He wears a leg brace to keep his foot raised. Without the brace, because of his drop foot, his walk is a slapping motion. He uses a cane, although he should use a walker—my opinion, our children's opinion, his physical therapist's opinion, not Henry's opinion. He uses that cane like a person with a broken leg using a pair of crutches, his whole body relying on one tiny rubber tip. We have a storage room full of walkers. Laurie orders one that seems perfect. Henry says no. Storage room. Laurie orders another one that really seems perfect. Henry says no. Storage room. Two years ago, he suffered a stroke, which left him with even more balance problems and mild cognitive impairment. Moving into Sharon Towers would mean greater independence for him. He could walk in the pool, do physical therapy in the exercise room, attend lectures right in the building, sit in the library and chat with whoever shows up.

Good, because, really, we'd be set for the future.

Not such a good thing, in that we'd be moving farther away from Laurie and Mike and their families. Now, Mike and his family are four minutes away from us; Laurie and her family, seven minutes away. If we move to Sharon Towers, we'd be in the SouthPark Mall area, which is busy, busy, heavy traffic, not the quiet neighborhood we live in (and I take walks in) now. During rush hour, it could be a thirty-minute drive for Laurie and Mike. And it's not an area they frequent, so they wouldn't just pop in, like they do now.

Not good to move anywhere, really, because we have set places for our belongings. We keep our keys in the little bird cup beside the coffeemaker, our batteries in a wire basket in the laundry room, and in my nightgown drawer, the eleven-inch-long, fish-shaped "scarf" our granddaughter, Lucy, knitted for me when she was nine. Every few years, I pull it out and show it to her. (She's now knitting blankets.) If we move, we'll have to get used to new places for our things. Not a major problem, of course, but still, not easy for old people. I picture us wandering through the rooms of our new apartment at Sharon Towers—*Where's the Scotch tape? Where'd we put the eye drops?*

Not good, because, while we reduced our living space by half when we moved from our house to our condo, we'd be downsizing even more. We'd share a closet. Not many walls for our paintings. Where would we keep our suitcases?

———

It's just so hard to imagine a place where you've never lived. You try to bring to life what it would be like. But it stays stubbornly abstract.

As I write these words, it grows clearer and clearer that my obsession over where we should live is all about Henry and me aging—my way of trying to make the big uncertainty in our lives certain. It's much less stressful to worry about our living situation than about our decline. If we make a decision about where we should live, then we've harnessed one slippery thing.

I am the least qualified person on earth to handle life's impermanence. Everything about me cries out for permanence. I like precision, but old age is sketchy. Life for an eighty-year-old and an eighty-two-year-old is not going to be static. Random chance is what it's all about. We're at the *mercy* of chance. I'm afraid I'm denying reality by not planning better for our future. But what does planning better for our future *mean*?

Mike believes we should make the move to Sharon Towers. However, he says, he could easily be talked into changing his mind. Laurie believes we should stay put. However, she says, she could easily be talked into changing her mind. Laurie is thinking best-case scenario. Mike is thinking worst-case scenario. Mike is a planner. Laurie is spontaneous.

Maybe, just maybe, there is no bad decision. It's just that: a decision.

Still, if we choose to go one way, will we harbor regrets over rejecting the other? Will we make a decision by simply not making a decision? Will we end up being sorry for what we've brought about?

Isn't this the way we felt every time we tried to decide where we should live next? How these housing decisions leave us feeling unmoored—or locked in. We begin to think a simple move is an action that can decide a life forever.

Let me say it again: We are hazy echoes of our former selves. We may look different, but inside we're still weighing the same old options. Just move the pieces around and see the patterns. The messy, complicated questions we faced when we were young foreshadow the messy, complicated questions we must come to grips with now. What counted then counts now. Heck, I'm still Judy Kurtz, the little girl who fell asleep to the hum of the attic fan, that cool breath ever so lightly brushing my cheek.

# 6.

My Breakfast Group has been meeting every Wednesday morning since 1985. In the beginning, we were four: Dannye, Ann, Bobbie, and me. We started meeting when Dannye, book editor of *The Charlotte Observer*, was writing a series on breakfast places in town, and she asked us to join her. We sampled one restaurant, then another, the only requirement being that we each order a different dish, then voice our opinions as to how the meal stacked up. After Dannye finished the series, we just kept meeting. We'd find a restaurant that suited us and meet there every week until it went out of business. Then on to the next.

We took in one new person, Clarissa; then another, Mary Hunter; and another, Laurie J., until we were seven. Our husbands grew close and formed a Tuesday lunch group that still meets.

Years passed. We grew older. Clarissa died of mantle cell lymphoma. Mary Hunter died of lung cancer. Ann moved to Charleston to be closer to her children and grandson. We took in Trisha. Now we are five, and we meet every week in Dannye's corner bungalow with the white picket fence.

For years, we met at seven-thirty, because some of us worked. Then we moved to eight o'clock, then nine. Now we meet at ten. Regardless of the time or place, regardless of how many we are, the ones we've lost, the ones we've gained, you'll find us every Wednesday morning listening hard to whoever is talking, then chiming in with our wisdoms.

In a column in *The Charlotte Observer* in 1995, after we'd been meeting for ten years, Dannye wrote this about the Breakfast Group: "Have we had spats and misunderstandings? A few. But we don't nurse grudges, and it's not in our nature to pout. What we do nurse is our habit of getting together, of hearing each other's stories, decoding each other's issues. As we hear and attend to each other, we rediscover and come to more fully understand ourselves."

Even though we're the Breakfast Group, we don't eat breakfast at our meetings anymore. We don't even have coffee. Two of us have a glass of water, one with ice. We sit in Dannye's living room, two matching love seats, wing chairs completing the circle, a mannequin in a wide-brimmed hat and white vintage dress looking on from the side, members of the group randomly telling what we have to tell. We have no agenda. Someone will bring up a concern—a child, a grandchild, a husband. Or someone will raise an interesting question about life. Or recommend a book or a TV series or a shampoo. (We talk a lot about hair.) We give sympathy and advice. Sometimes we skip the sympathy and go straight to advice. Sometimes the person with the problem is disappointed when she receives only advice, no sympathy. We tell about family trips, family illnesses, family conversations, and, always, how holiday dinners go. We've been through parents' illnesses and deaths, a divorce and dating again, children going to college, children moving back home, children moving on and marrying and having children, children's marriages in trouble, children's divorces, children's successes, sick spouses, a spouse dying, our own breast cancer, arthritis, surgery on knees and shoulders and feet and faces, a child dying. Our lives are linked through these life changes. We haul out our favorite quotes when someone needs bolstering. Our all-time favorite: "You're only as happy as your unhappiest child." My personal favorite: "It really is as hard as you think it is."

If a person is not talking much, someone will say, "Hey, what's going on?"

It's 2021, and I'm being quiet. So, someone asks, "Judy, how are things with you?'

I say that I'm writing a new book.

They ask what it's about.

"Aging," I say. "What it's like to turn eighty."

I tell how many pages I'm up to: 125! Beginning my writing career as a poet made me page obsessed. I'm always amazed I can come up with enough words to fill more than a hundred sheets of paper. When I switched from the brevity of poetry to the long haul of novel writing, I conducted research for several Sundays, scanning *The New York Times Book Review* to see how short a novel could be and still be called a novel. I found one that was only 206 pages. *Aha! I just need to make it to 206!* When I would run into someone I knew in the produce aisle of the grocery store and that person asked what I was working on, my answer was "I'm writing a 206-page novel."

I tell the Breakfast Group a little more about my new memoir, then look around the living room at the faces that appear the same to me as when we began meeting thirty-seven years ago—the way we superimpose familiar young faces onto old faces, past versions of ourselves still everywhere.

Dannye, eighty—gifted poet and retired journalist, small, wears what you'd imagine a poet would wear (shawls and scarves), makes us laugh with her humor, longtime second marriage after divorce from first husband, two grown sons in town, three grandchildren, three great-grandchildren.

Trisha, eighty—retired certified financial planner, volunteers as a math tutor in the public schools, even smaller than Dannye, buys her pajamas in the children's department, pragmatic *and* a sparkling smile, longtime second marriage after divorce from first husband, married daughter in town, three grandchildren.

Laurie J., seventy-nine—must have been a beautiful teenager because she's beautiful now, earned a master's in social work, retired mediator, renovated and sold old houses (she and her female partners did the work themselves), artist, son married with two daughters in Oregon, married daughter died of bile duct cancer in 2020.

Bobbie, seventy-eight—retired from nonprofit work, cares deeply about injustice and doing what she can to end it, campaigns for Democratic candidates, poet, disarmingly honest and witty, two married sons (one with three sons in Charlotte, one in Montana). Bobbie is the only widow in our group. Her husband died from complications of Alzheimer's in 2018.

———

"What are *your* thoughts on aging?" I ask no one in particular, everyone, really.

"We're all gonna die," Dannye blurts out.

She gets our attention. Several of us say something funny in response, but because we all talk at once, I can't hear individual voices.

Dannye goes on: "I'm not a morbid person. Y'all know that. But I think I really take it in now. That I'm going to die. And I think about it every day."

She says she feels that times were happier and fuller in the past, more peopled. Not that she's *un*happy now. It's just that her life is less crowded, and feels vacant. Maybe, she says, the pandemic is partly to blame.

"Don't y'all feel lonely?" she asks, looking around at each of us.

I nod yes. Not sure if anyone else nods yes.

"I don't know that I feel lonely," Laurie J. says. "I think I feel adrift."

Maybe lonely and adrift are the same thing. Maybe an extroverted old person (Dannye) feels lonely, and an introverted old person (Laurie J.) feels adrift.

"But it seems like"—Dannye again—"in the past, there were more times that were just *happy*. Because I have these lonely feelings now, images from the past—small moments—pop up for me all the time. I can see the scenes so clearly, as though they just happened."

Bobbie says her life is much happier now that she's older. She says there's a curiosity in her, an excitement to experience new things, a self-confidence she didn't have when she was younger. "For example," she says, "I never imagined I would sing in the church choir!" She sees these years as the best in her life.

Laurie J. says that the night before her daughter, Paige, died of cancer, Paige told her, "I don't feel like I'm going to die." Laurie J. says she thinks we all feel that way. That we don't believe we're going to die. We think we'll just keep on living.

Then she adds, "Here's what it is about aging: There are a lot of things I used to do that I don't want to do anymore. But I really miss *wanting* to do them. Like skiing. Or traveling to ... Scandinavia. And, oh my gosh, sex! John and I used to have so much fun, just playing! I miss the longing. The passion ... for so many things."

So far, Trisha has not said anything. Not unusual for Trisha. She often waits until everyone else has weighed in before she speaks. But then, when she does voice an opinion, we appreciate her insight. I turn to her. "Trisha, how 'bout you?"

"I don't think about aging. Ever," she says. "It's just not something that crosses my mind. I have the same energy I've always had. I feel as young as I did thirty years ago." Trisha's mother lived to a hundred, and her mind was sharp almost to the end—worked crossword puzzles, played Words with Friends online. So, eighty probably feels like middle age to Trisha.

"I like *now* a lot," she adds. "I'm much more *regularly* kind, more *regularly* thoughtful. I look back at my twenty-five years in business. Every day you had to make more money for the company. They posted it on the wall, how much business each financial advisor transacted that day. I may be competitive, but that was too much even for me. It felt like I was constantly being judged. Oh my God, in retrospect, I realize I hated it. I don't miss it at all. No comparison between my life now and my life then."

I believe it's possible to hold contradictory thoughts in your head. Which is to say, I feel the same as each of my friends.

Like Laurie J., I remember how great it was to travel. Henry and I skied in Norway, hiked in Wyoming, flew to France twice one year. But then I think about the hassle of flying and boarding passes and taking your shoes off in the airport. I think about how ski boots never fit right, how you had to lug those heavy skis and poles around. I think about how the friend who led your hike was always surprised that the trail was steeper and had a bigger drop-off than he'd remembered. I'm not sorry those days are gone. But I did love being excited about them. Well, like Laurie J., I miss wanting all that.

Like Trisha, I can go days not thinking of aging. I forget I'm old.

And yet, like Dannye, I obsess about being old. When Henry and I moved from our house to our condo, I pared down way too dramatically. I made Henry get rid of all his binoculars. He was hell-bent to keep them, but if *he* couldn't have them, he wanted our grown children to have them. He kept asking, didn't they want some binoculars for concerts? ("Dad, nobody uses binoculars at concerts!") I gave away my Bundt pan. Did I think I was done making cakes? We donated hundreds of books to the library for their sale. Back and forth I went, to Goodwill and Habitat for Humanity. I left overstuffed bags on the porch for the Kidney Foundation. My thinking was, I didn't want our children to be stuck with our stuff after we died. As though death was coming up any minute. As though we were moving into hospice.

I'm also right there with Dannye and her pop-up visions from days gone by. Jumping era to era. Memories like a dotted line. Here an image, there an image. Little capsules. How, at this age, we never get sick of stories from the past. We're pulled back into a moment and see a younger self, as though we're spotting someone we used to know.

And I'm like Bobbie, feeling I'm so much more complete now, less conflicted about who I might be. (Aren't I already who I might be?) I do think aging has brought a greater understanding of the most obscure parts of myself. Mediocrity was never my goal, but as I get closer to the end, I find that perfection is not all it's cracked up to be. *Done is better than perfect.* Maybe I'm just settling into myself, learning to be okay with the difference between what is true and what I wish were true.

# 7.

The first week of June 1963, I graduated from the University of Georgia and called off my wedding, which was set to take place three weeks later. My engagement was not to Henry, whom I would meet four years later. (My on-then-off engagement is another genesis story I've told over and over, in just about every book I've written. As though if I tell it often enough, I'll finally understand how I could have done something like that.)

You realize, of course, three weeks before the wedding is very close to the big day. Invitations had been mailed and gifts were arriving— dinner plates, silver forks and spoons, ice buckets. A white, lacy wedding gown and veil hung in my closet. I'd bought eight beaded evening bags to give to my eight bridesmaids. (I'll never run out of beaded evening bags!) My fiancé and I had put down a deposit on a duplex in Chapel Hill, where he would begin law school in the fall and I'd teach high school English. He was a really good person; I just wasn't in love with him. Because I'd said yes when he gave me a diamond ring on my twenty-first birthday back in October, because I'd let eight months go by, because all that time I knew I should say *something* but didn't, I was hugely disappointed in myself. I spent the summer after breaking the engagement at home on Eden Terrace, living with my parents, conscience-stricken and depressed, unsure what would come next in my life.

Early August, a college friend, Susan, called. She knew of my abrupt change of plans and asked if I'd like to share an apartment with her on Peachtree Road in Atlanta. I said yes and immediately started looking for a teaching job. The future felt suddenly open. Everything possible.

I was so late applying, though, most schools had already hired the staff they needed for fall. Roosevelt High School, the largest high school for white students in Atlanta, located in one of the most disadvantaged neighborhoods, had just been court-ordered to admit Black students. Roosevelt would be one of the first high schools in the South to integrate. Teachers who'd taught there for years were handing in their resignations. People applying for jobs were steering clear of the school and the turmoil that would surely ensue. Atlanta City Schools was frantic to fill the vacant positions.

Here comes Judy, newly free, having been told over and over how brave she was to end an engagement. In truth, I did do something difficult—well, you could also call it insensitive: I hurt another person. But bravery is what most people who knew me focused on. Did that mean I was now ready to take on the world and make my mark? I knew teaching at Roosevelt *that* year would have a courage and a genuineness to it, knew that teaching in a low-income school the first year of integration in Georgia had a sense of rightness to it. But I'd never seen myself as the heroic type. And oh, those images on the nightly news of random schools across the country integrating. The chaos. Violence. Bloodshed. I was, for sure, not entering a neutral situation.

In the end, though, I knew where I needed to be.

I signed on to teach eighth and ninth grade English at Roosevelt. Because my resume stated I'd been editor of my high school newspaper, Mr. Baxter, the pale, desperate principal who hired me, insisted I also teach journalism. In fact, I had planned to major in journalism in college, but when I found out the labs were at 8 a.m., I switched my major to education and English. I never took the first journalism class. Had no experience or training whatsoever to *teach* it. That would not be the only part of this job I wasn't prepared for.

--------

My first morning, I pulled into the faculty parking lot. Patrol cars lined the curb in front of the school. The opening bell had not rung yet; it was still early. Had something bad already happened?

I shifted my books and papers close to my chest and pulled open the heavy front door of the school. Students were bustling about, calling out to each other, laughing, teasing, moving through the halls in packs, finding their homerooms. It all appeared normal. Even smelled the way I remembered school smelling—linoleum floors mopped and waxed, chalk dust, pencil lead and new three-ring notebooks, kids. I was five-two, weighed a hundred and five. I saw right away that I was smaller than most of the students. *Maybe I should've worn heels instead of loafers and socks.*

All of a sudden, my attention was drawn to a policeman standing beside the marble stairs, his eyes fixed on some distant thing. He was fingering a gun buckled to his side. I had never seen a gun in real life. I stopped cold and stared, riveted. I could see the trigger. I imagined a finger slowly pulling it.

But then I snapped back and realized I needed to move on. I spotted another policeman down the hall, outside Mr. Baxter's office. Another gun. *Keep going, Judy.* I circled around the first policeman at the staircase, a wide circle, and headed up the steps to my homeroom. On the second floor, another policeman stood guard, arms pressed to his sides. When I reached the third floor, another police-man. I was breathless, maybe from climbing the stairs, maybe from all those policemen, maybe from all those guns. But I smiled at this policeman and said, "Good morning." I imagine now that his eyes darted left and right. Maybe he nodded. I wondered if integration was something these policemen believed in. Or something they were dead set against. Or was this just another day on the job?

————

First-period English class, around twenty-five ninth graders, two Black students in the class, one girl and one boy, side by side in the front row, inches from where I stood. (In every one of my classes, the one or two Black students sat up front.) I read aloud a short story about a British teenager who was plucked from his low-rung position in life to meet the queen. After I finished reading, I asked the students to name an important person they'd like to meet and tell why.

A white boy's hand shot up. He was seated at a desk way over to the side.

"I wish I could meet President Kennedy," he blurted out, twist-ing his skinny shoulders to look around the room, making sure all eyes were fastened on him. "I'd tell him to get these niggas out of our school!"

My eyes immediately took in the room. I felt the hush more than I could actually hear it. Like a vibration.

Did all the white students feel this way? I couldn't tell by looking at their faces. Such faint, vacant stares. And what were the two Black students thinking? All I saw there was a tense blankness.

I tried to rearrange my own face to hide my panic. I tried to think what I could possibly say. I'd known these kids maybe thirty minutes.

"What's your name?" I said to the boy who'd just flipped my first day of teaching on its back.

"Freddy." Spoken as though he was proud to claim what he'd done.

I don't remember what I said next. I just know my response was short. And stiff. And inadequate. It went something like this:

"Well, Freddy, I'm going to pretend I didn't hear you say that. I'm going to assume everyone in this room wants to live peacefully with each other and we're going to do our best toward that goal."

What I said was ridiculous. For days afterward, I replayed the scene in my mind and thought of all the things I *should* have said.

*You will not say anything like that in this room ever again! Not ever! That kind of talk will not be tolerated in my class! Got that, kid?*

*Let's go, Freddy. You're outta here! I'm taking you down to the principal's office! Now!*

Plenty I could have said.

But then I needed to figure out how to fill the remaining minutes in class.

My hands were shaking, my voice tinny as I went around the room, up one row, down the next, asking each student my original question: What famous person would you like to meet and why? We went from Lou Gehrig to Helen Keller to some singer in a band I'd never heard of. The room was like a held breath. Until the bell finally rang and we moved on to second period.

————

A couple of months in, the situation was calm, and the policemen had disappeared from the hallways. My days at Roosevelt High School were moving along uneventfully.

One morning, late October, beginning of eighth grade homeroom,

I heard noises in the cloakroom. The usual noises, yes—students hanging up their jackets, talking, laughing. Maybe some noises I didn't usually hear, I wasn't sure. Scuffling, I thought. Grunts? But it was noisy in the classroom, too—students bursting in, jabbering, dropping notebooks, scraping chairs. I didn't pay much attention to what might be happening in the cloakroom.

Then—maybe I should go check.

I started toward the sounds. I got as far as the doorway between the classroom and the cloakroom.

Stop. Focus.

Two husky boys—one white, one Black—appeared to be wrestling in that narrow space, locked tight, knocking each other over. Wait! They weren't playing! It was a fight! The freight of their bodies, now both on the floor, a hand reaching for a neck, a hand reaching for a pant leg, the two of them rolling around, the sound of it, just bodies, thunking, blundering, no voices, one boy on top, the other on top. I saw punching, but I couldn't tell who was doing the punching and who was being punched. They were just struggling against each other, some crazy momentum dragging the two of them across the linoleum floor.

I think other students hovered close by. And then maybe more students piled into the cloakroom. But I don't know what they were doing, whether they were shouting or silent. It was like a bomb had gone off in my stomach or my chest or my head, and all I could see and hear were the two boys.

I had to do *something*.

Just jump in? How to do that?

I planted my feet and reached way over, my arms wedged together from my elbows to my fingertips like a pole or a rod, pushing in. But I was not accomplishing a thing. Could not begin to get my skinny arms between them. Not enough strength. Those boys were so big and so pinned together. Then I maneuvered my whole body in, shoved myself right into the middle of them, the three of us now a clenched mass. Like I'd joined the fight. Like we were stuck together. But I just kept shoving, shoving, until, finally, I forced them apart, a space between those two bodies, one of my hands holding off the white boy, one hand holding off the Black boy, their T-shirts wadded up in my fingers. I clutched fabric as though I could keep them away from each other just by holding on.

Now all three of us were upright, standing there, nobody making a move.

"Okay, okay!" I said, trying to find a voice that sounded like a voice a teacher might use. Instead, my voice was so small it sounded like it came from miles away.

And then I looked down. Blood had dripped all over my loafers and socks. Blood?

I looked up. Blood. Both boys. Bloody.

The Black boy's cheek was split open, a jagged line from beneath his eye to the corner of his downturned mouth, skin zipped open. Just open! And the blood! The blood!

He wasn't crying. Maybe I heard him take a single scratchy breath. Maybe I didn't hear anything. His expression was—empty.

At that moment, I could not compute. My mind was searching for a narrative to explain. I knew what I was seeing, but I couldn't fully grasp it.

I heard myself breathing, in-out, in-out, as if I'd been running. I tried to ignore my heartbeat.

Out of the corner of my eye, I glimpsed the white boy's bare arm. His wrist. His hand. His bloody hand. The knife he was holding.

Was it a pocketknife? A kitchen knife? I'm sure I knew then what I was seeing, but it has since gone out of my head. All I remember is a blade. That's it. A blade.

I immediately whisked the Black boy down to the nurse's office. Back up the stairs—I picture myself taking them two at a time, but I would never have been able to do that—to my classroom to grab the white boy and get him down to the principal's office. Where'd the knife go? I should've taken the two of them together, not left the white boy behind. What was he doing when I left for the nurse's office? What did the rest of the kids do?

—————

Here's the incredible thing: There was no conversation in the teacher's lounge about what had happened, not a word—who started the fight, what the repercussions would be, a knife at school, punishment for the white kid, concern for the Black kid, this first-year teacher breaking up a knife fight, nothing. For sure, everyone had heard. News travels.

I didn't bring up any of this with my fellow teachers, not during breaks, not at lunch, not after school walking to our cars in the parking lot. I didn't mention it for two reasons: I believed I knew whose side most of the teachers (all of them white) would land on. And part of me felt guilty. I could have handled everything better. Been more forceful. Acted quicker. I don't know when during the fight the boy's face got cut, but maybe if I'd gone in sooner, been stronger, I could have kept it from happening.

I did ask Mr. Baxter what action would be taken. He skirted my question. That's when I knew there would be no punishment for the white boy. I didn't press.

To this day, I regret my passivity.

Time passed. Both boys remained in my homeroom, as if everything had been forgotten. As if that boy's face had not been stitched back together. As if I'd invented the whole thing out of thin air.

———

Then, it was a warm afternoon, November 22, 1963, last period of the day, still my first year at Roosevelt, journalism class, which was actually the school newspaper staff meeting. Mary, the editor—a twelfth grader, excellent student, white, one of the few who were trying to bring classmates together—began assigning articles. Through the tall, steep windows along one long wall, sunlight washed the room. This was always fun, seeing who would write which articles. Mary was interrupted by the static that always preceded an announcement over the loudspeaker. The static seemed to go on longer than usual, as though the whole system were clearing its throat.

Then, Mr. Baxter's voice: "Students and teachers of Roosevelt High . . . President Kennedy has been shot."

I don't remember if the principal said anything else. All I remember is the silence that followed his announcement. No one in the classroom made eye contact. Not the tiniest shift of breath.

Then suddenly, like an explosion, I heard students running out of their classrooms, up and down the hall, whooping, yelling, a splutter of feet and bodies and cheering—joyful cheering! *Joyful!* Like a celebration!

My classroom was then empty. I remember Mary still standing there, next to the windows, just standing there.

———

Here's where I go blank again. I can't remember what happened next. How did school end that day? Early dismissal? Were the students and faculty told to leave, Mr. Baxter suddenly everywhere? Police streaming in? What was it like when I walked out into the hall, down the stairs, out the front door? Were the students still running around, cheering? What was it like when we returned to school the next morning?

———

My brother, Donald, had a wide perspective from having grown up in Rock Hill and now having lived in New York City for many years. He was fascinated with my stories about my days at Roosevelt. Over and over, in every phone conversation, he tried to talk me into keeping a journal so that I could write a book or an op-ed piece or even just a letter to the editor of *The Atlanta Constitution*.

"This is history!" he said. "You have to write about it!" Every time we spoke, the same urging.

But I never made the first note.

Writing about integrating a school in the midst of integrating a school felt dangerous. The entire time I taught at Roosevelt, I was aware of the risks around me. First of all, I wasn't sure it was okay for an Atlanta teacher to write about the integration of her school. Was there some kind of policy I'd agreed to when I signed my contract? All those legal words I never even read. I know how crazy this sounds, but nothing seemed out of the question during those tumultuous times. Most important, how in the world could I possibly expose the prejudice I saw at Roosevelt—the students *and* the teachers? What if people I interacted with every day found out I'd written about them? What would they do? It was the first time in my sheltered life I'd found myself in a situation that threatened, minute by minute, to turn perilous. I was so inexperienced. In everything.

I'd been brave enough to break an engagement. But, really, was that bravery? At that time, at that point, the most I could say was that I left.

I'd been brave enough to teach in a school most teachers were avoiding. I was brave enough to break up a knife fight. But was it bravery? At that time, at that point, the most I could say was that I stayed.

Oh, the fast heartbeat I felt so much of my time at Roosevelt High. Such a volatile situation. I was scared for my personal safety, scared for the safety of the Black students—those few boys and girls so carefully selected, star pupils plucked from their all-Black schools and deposited in classrooms at white Roosevelt, coached to handle an impossible situation, how unwelcome they were. I was scared for the world, which seemed to be splitting apart.

How was I to take on this broken world? Make my mark? There were limits all around me. And because of how unready I was to face such a volatile situation, I also became aware of the limits within myself.

———

Old age is a volatile situation, too. When I make this comparison, I don't mean to minimize the staggering, ongoing, real-life problem of racism. What I mean is, I learned that every day I climbed those marble stairs to my classroom, anything could happen. Some stray shock.

And now, at eighty, when I open my eyes to a new day, I understand that anything can happen. I am as unprepared for what is before me as I was the first year I taught. The tension of not knowing when the unexpected will invade. Something coming out of nowhere. Lurking danger. Always, the possibility of a stroke, heart attack, dementia, cancer, a fall and a fractured something. I read the obituaries in the paper—all those people who married the love of their lives, who never met a stranger—and when they're younger than me, I either feel relieved (I'm beating the odds) or I worry I'm past due. When they're older, I either feel relieved (I've got time) or I worry I will never make it to an advanced age. Maybe this afternoon I'll drop dead on my living room rug. Maybe I'll make it to a hundred and get a phone call from the president. Maybe I'll suffer for years and, when I finally close my eyes for good, my loved ones will be relieved.

Of course, old age also offers the promise of being exactly where I need to be—similar to my years at Roosevelt High School. When the pendulum swings us into a new place so stripped of familiarity and protection, it is possible for us to upend our limited ways of understanding and our ground-in cowardice. Maybe even find inklings of courage. Life can be a continuous act of creativity—if we look at it with a frank eye.

# 8.

I was twenty-three when I made another big-time move toward the unfamiliar. I packed a bag and boarded Eastern Airlines, unsure where I'd ultimately live and work, or whom I'd meet. I embraced the raw astonishment of abandoning the life I knew for...one I didn't know.

It was 1965. I'd taught at Roosevelt two years, loved my job, assumed I'd teach until retirement, maybe receive a watch or gift certificate from Rich's Department Store from Mr. Baxter in a ceremony in our drafty old gym where I'd sat in the shaky wooden bleachers with the other teachers, surrounded by students cheering for our basketball team. Now they would be cheering for me and all the years I'd climbed the stairs to my room, all the years I'd taken roll, assigned book reports on *David Copperfield*, graded tests, diagrammed prepositional phrases on the board.

I did not spend the rest of my life at Roosevelt. My friend from college, Thea, gutsy Thea, was talking, endlessly, about moving to New York City—and why didn't I go, too? The picture she painted was convincing: We'd find glamour jobs you could only find in New York City, we'd meet great guys in neighborhood bars, we'd get blond highlights in our hair. I was seeing possibilities. We reserved a double room at the Barbizon Hotel for Women for one month, just until we could rent a cool apartment. I was growing more and more excited. Skyscrapers! Statue of Liberty! Subways!

A week before we planned to meet at LaGuardia, she called.

"Judy, I won't be going to New York, after all. Howie and I are getting married."

Howie had been her boyfriend since our senior year at the University of Georgia, when he'd been at the Naval Academy in Athens. But it was an on-again, off-again romance. And it had been off for quite a while.

"No, no, you *aren't* getting married!" I cried. "You're moving to New York! With me! You can always get married! You can't always live in New York!"

Now I realize I never even asked what had transpired in their relationship, why the change. I never even congratulated her or said I was happy for her. I was hell-bent on changing her mind. She was hell-bent on marrying.

We hung up. A minute passed, then another. I told myself to breathe, long and slow. Now what? I could look back at the past months and see the dominoes falling. I'd already given notice at Roosevelt; everything was in motion. Too late to switch course. Nothing for me to do but go. I would just be a different kind of person—the kind of person who ups and moves to New York City, alone. I switched the reservation at the Barbizon to a single.

To add to my aloneness, Donald, who could be affectionate and attentive, whose presence had helped assuage Mother's worries about my moving ("Your brother is right there in Manhattan—just in case you need somebody."), whose presence also had helped assuage my worries, chose my moving day to travel to France's wine country for a month. Not unusual for him. He could disappear, his affection and attention a little unreliable. So yes, I had a brother in New York; I wasn't totally alone. But really, I was totally alone.

———

I tell people I'm a person who chooses the safe and familiar. Staying right where I am, isn't that what I like to do? As if I want to arrive at death wrapped in comfort, protected, nothing unfamiliar or unsound ever having gotten close. Oh, I know people who seek adventure. I married one. Gave birth to two. My husband, daughter, and son don't miss a thing. I've always seen myself as being just fine with missing.

But how well do we really know ourselves? Maybe we're braver than we think. Maybe when we take a closer look at how we operate in the world, we see that we *are* capable of signing on for the unexpected. Maybe we do barrel on, enter new territory, cut loose from the place we know.

———

Early September, I arrived at that Italian Renaissance residential hotel at Lexington Avenue and 63rd Street. It was one of those golden Manhattan days, seventy degrees, not a cloud. The minute I paid the cab driver, pushed through the revolving doors of the Barbizon, and crossed the lobby to the front desk—my heels clicking—I felt primed, already in that space where the mind is starting to invent who to be next. I could almost feel it, a shift of gravity.

My room was so tiny I could lie in bed and open my door at the same time. The faded flowered blue bedspread matched the faded flowered blue curtains. I raised the window shade all the way up to check out my view: gray buildings and iron fire escapes. I unpacked, then headed out to stroll around the neighborhood—63rd Street, 62nd, up to 64th, 65th, over to Park Avenue, 5th. I needed to figure out where I was, learn the landscape. I needed to turn a city as unfamiliar to me as Spokane or Singapore into home. (My parents had taken Brenda and me to New York City once, to experience the 1952 presidential election in Times Square, and my cousin Debbie and I had spent a weekend with Donald when we were in college. That's all I knew of the city.)

I passed a Horn & Hardart Automat, peeked in, the wall of little glass boxes like a post office of food. Bloomingdales! The skinny mannequins in the windows, velvet bell-bottoms. Chock Full o'Nuts, a poster outside showing their famous cream cheese and nut sandwich on dark raisin bread. I started walking faster, falling in with everyone hurrying somewhere on those busy streets. The sun felt warm and good on my face.

Back at the Barbizon, still my first day, I knocked on the dark, ornate doors lining my hall, just to introduce myself to my neighbors, say hello. I will never forget the look on their faces, although I really couldn't see their faces behind the doors they barely opened. In the South, it's what you do; you meet your neighbors. At the Barbizon, I now knew, you didn't.

Many of the residents were students at Katharine Gibbs, the elite secretarial school with the famous dress code—suits, hats, and short, white cotton gloves. The Barbizon had its own strict rules: No men allowed above the ground floor. No shorts, pants, or jeans in the lobby. That's just how it was then. My junior year at the University of Georgia, I had been suspended for two weeks—sent home!—when the dean of women caught me wearing Bermuda shorts in public.

In that way that Donald could surprise me with his attention, he gave me a welcome-to-New York present when he returned from France: a day at Kenneth, the Upper East Side salon owned by Mr. Kenneth, who was famous for doing Jackie Kennedy's hair. Also, Marilyn Monroe's and Audrey Hepburn's. I tried to act as though I felt right at home in that hushed and perfumed salon, its plush flowered carpeting, red-and-yellow-paisley everything. *Oh sure, a total makeover—haircut and styling, blond highlights, manicure, makeup lesson—I've done all this before! A thousand places like this in Rock Hill!* I added false eyelashes and little tins of taupe and alabaster eye shadow to Donald's tab.

Now it was time to think about a job. I was determined to find something sophisticated—hopefully in show business.

I answered an ad in *The New York Times* to work at Filmex, a company that produced TV commercials. Not exactly showbiz. But compared to teaching nouns and verbs to eighth and ninth graders, it was showbiz enough. My job description: assistant to Natalie K. Noreen (thin-lipped, straight-backed, and humorless, so imperious she used the K). She was an assistant to Alejandro D'Antonio, a producer. In other words, I was an assistant to an assistant. The bike courier and I occupied the lowliest positions in the company.

My job included bartending in the president's suite when advertising executives came to film. The night before I reported for work, I studied a how-to-mix-cocktails book. I was ready for anything— martinis, white Russians, vodka gimlets.

My job also included relieving Madelyn, the switchboard operator with the posh British accent, at lunch. Which meant that when a call came in for one of the crew filming in the studio, I had to page them over the PA. My first day, I pushed the button, paged a cameraman, heard my voice reverberate through the building. *Good*, I thought,

*I'm doing it right.* Minutes later, the cameraman called, said something might be wrong with the system and would I count slowly over the PA from one to ten.

"Sure," I said. Miss Eager To Please. "One. Two. Three. Four. Five. Six. Seven. Eight. Nine. Ten."

"Great," came the next call. "Now, honey, would you count backwards, from ten to one?"

I stopped at eight. When I heard laughter pouring from the studio. Of course! My voice was thick with South Carolina!

I soon became friends with the guys in the studio. I loved being on set, close to the actors and cameras and cables and lights.

One morning they were shooting a TV commercial for Top Job Heavy Duty Cleanser, and the hand model didn't show up. They asked me to fill in. I was thrilled. Me—on the right side of the camera. Although all you could see was my hand. It turned out to be really hard work, my elbow resting on the table, my hand in the air, fingers tight around a full thirty-two-ounce bottle of cleaner, shot after shot (was it hour after hour?), keeping my Top Job from tipping over.

I'd worked at Filmex maybe two months when the first and biggest New York power failure in history occurred. Around five thirty, just before we would leave for home, everything went dark. I found out later that my mother, hearing the news, was frantic to find out if I was safe. I was more than safe. The entire office emptied out into the street and over to "our" bar, where we drank and partied until late. Three women from work who couldn't get home to Brooklyn walked the twenty-two blocks with me to my apartment to spend the night. (I'd moved from the Barbizon into an apartment with a woman I'd known in college.) The city—at three in the morning—was alive with big groups of people moving along the sidewalks.

My job at Filmex was not without its minuses. The men who worked there, including the studio crew, never bothered to learn my name.

"Hon, go to the supply room and grab a roll of film!"

"Sweetheart, get so-and-so on the phone!"

As naive as I was, and even though the culture had barely begun to acknowledge the bad behavior of some men, I knew the climate at Filmex was not right. Men came on to the women who worked there. One night, after an office party, my boss's boss, Alejandro, offered to drop me at my apartment in a cab. He was a happy-go-lucky kind of guy, known for his big laugh and the khaki safari jacket he always wore, regardless of the weather. My immediate boss, Natalie K. Noreen, kept him in line. But Natalie K. Noreen was not present that evening. And I wasn't about to make a fuss. So, fine, I made out with him in the back seat of the cab. Next day at work, he still didn't know my name.

After a few months, the president of Filmex, Robert Bergman, lost yet another secretary—he was not easy to work for—and I slipped into that position. Definitely a promotion. No longer an assistant to an assistant, I was now a full-fledged secretary. A move from the slightly seedy studio to the plush executive offices one block away, near the United Nations building. This put me even closer to glamour; Mr. Bergman's son was married to Judy Carne, the "sock it to me" star of the TV show *Laugh-In.* (Later she would marry Burt Reynolds.) I was dizzy with proximity to celebrity.

I had lied in my initial interview about being able to take dictation, and while it hadn't mattered in my first position, in my new position it did. So, I devised a strategy. When I took dictation from Mr. Bergman, I wrote down the first letter of every word. Then I raced back to my desk, just outside his door, to type, quick, before I forgot what the letters stood for. If the phone rang, I let it ring. If someone needed to talk with me, I waved them off. If I couldn't remember some of the words, I guessed. But I'd majored in English. I'd taught English. I certainly knew how to write a letter. In fact, it was the word *certainly* that tripped me up, as in *I certainly hope to hear from you soon.*

"That's not what I said." Mr. Bergman—his normally hard-to-read, stagy face now mad-red—was pointing to the sentence where I'd winged it. "This does not sound like me. I would never use the word *certainly.*"

Because Filmex's executive offices were located in a luxury apartment building, Mr. Bergman's office was actually a spacious primary bedroom with a large adjoining bathroom. He kept his files in a jumble in the bathtub. As if *certainly* wasn't enough, when he left for a business trip to Los Angeles, I organized those files. He was livid, reddening, again: "What right do you have to go through my files? I can't find anything."

Next: a demotion. I was still a secretary, only now it was to the vice president, Peter Griffith. I felt embarrassed getting fired, but my new position seemed promising. I was even closer to glamour. Mr. Griffith was the ex-husband of Tippi Hedren and the father of Melanie Griffith. He'd been a child movie star and was the best-looking man I'd ever seen in person. I could hardly do my job for looking at that perfectly symmetrical, perfectly beautiful face. I was thrilled when Tippi Hedren called. I pictured her running from all those birds in her Hitchcock movie. But no amount of being starstruck qualified me to be an executive secretary.

And there was that same prefeminism denigration of women throughout Filmex.

Advertising people who shot commercials at Filmex seemed different. They were respectful, and they spoke like English majors. Because they probably *had* been English majors. I'd always liked to write; I wondered if I could get a job as a copywriter in an ad agency.

This time, instead of answering an ad in *The New York Times*, I went through an employment agency. Because I was a woman, though, and women always started as secretaries, the only job I qualified for was . . . secretary.

Next job: secretary to Ted Shaw, head copywriter on the American Express and Shell Oil accounts at the international ad agency, Ogilvy & Mather, founded by David Ogilvy, a Londoner known as the "father of advertising." David Ogilvy had just written the best-seller, *Confessions of an Advertising Man*.

Before I'd reported to work at Filmex, I'd studied cocktails. This time, it was Ogilvy's book on advertising.

My first day at work, David Ogilvy happened to be in the New York office. He was mostly based in the London office, so when he came to New York, the entire agency—both floors—was abuzz. I was typing an ad for Ted when a shadow crossed my desk. I looked up and there was David Ogilvy himself, maybe in his fifties, smoking his pipe. He was dressed so elegantly he could have been a suit ad for Bloomingdales. Ogilvy himself, perched on my desk! In his cultured British accent, he welcomed me to Ogilvy & Mather. I told him how much I loved his book. He stayed right there, inches away, and we chatted, on and on. I could see Pepi, the older, gray-haired secretary whose desk was behind mine, who'd worked at Ogilvy & Mather for years. She was not typing, just staring. Pepi and I could not have been more awed if London had sent over Princess Margaret.

Ted, my boss, was easygoing, intelligent, generous about teaching me copywriting. If there was a product to be named, he brought me into the brainstorming session. A small print ad or thirty-second commercial: *Let's see what you can do, Judy.*

———

It wasn't long before I started dating one of the chief executives at Ogilvy. Unfortunately, he was married. But that didn't stop me. Because he was from London, because he was older and charming, big-shouldered and strapping, because we did not have sex—we did a lot of kissing—our romance felt okay to me. How easy it is to succumb to rationalization when you dodge a few details. Our "romance" began with dancing at an office party. Then he took me to trendy nightclubs. We just kept dancing. And kissing. "The More I See You" was *the* song that summer; I thought of it as *our* song. For a girl from Rock Hill, this was not a turn I'd ever expected in my life. Not the British part. Not the married man part. Not the fancy nightclub part. One night, after work and before a nightclub, we stopped off at his apartment on Central Park South for him to pick up something. His wife and kids were at their summer house in the Hamptons. There, on the piano, were silver-framed photographs of that wife and those children. Their faces. Like any family. It could have been *my* family. Something flipped over inside me. That moment, before we left for the nightclub, I ended it.

Then I started seeing Dan, a copywriter in Ted's group. Not married. My age. Preppy, navy blazer, pocket handkerchief, good-looking, clever. Dan would stop by my desk and flirt. Around that time, I read that Helen Gurley Brown, who'd revived the magazine *Cosmopolitan*, said something like this in an interview: "There's nothing particularly attractive about a thirty-eight-year-old virgin." I was twenty-four—fourteen years to go—but I took her words to heart. I bought black lace underwear and made the decision to have sex with Dan. You would not find me at age thirty-eight still a virgin. Maybe I was just determined to rid myself of latticed southernness, small town—ness, naivete.

It was odd, sleeping at Dan's. His apartment was generically furnished and tidy; he always served red wine, brie, and crackers. But I'd never spent that much time in a man's apartment, had never begun the day in a man's bed. Even odder, I remember very little about sex with him. My main memory is that the two of us made up his double bed in the morning, him on one side, me on the other. We fluffed the pillows, smoothed the bottom sheet, folded the hem of the top sheet over the blanket. He was neater than I was, so he would say, "No, do it this way." Shouldn't he just make up his own bed? And why is that all I remember?

I was also dating other guys. Stu was older (forty?), with black-rimmed glasses and a confident, moneyed manner. We saw Broadway shows and sat at the head table at political fundraisers. We had nothing in common. I also dated wiry, chain-smoking Wally, who worked in shipping at Ogilvy. He smelled like the Winstons he kept in his shirt pocket. I think we mostly went out for coffee. My friend Marsha, who worked a floor above me at Ogilvy and later married Neil Diamond after he'd divorced his first wife, fixed me up with her ex-boyfriend, whose name is lost to me. He had long hair, tied back. We dated for months; I wondered what it would be like to marry him. I also really liked Ben—so tall, dark, and handsome, women on the street turned to stare at him. Ben's job at the William Morris Talent Agency was escorting celebrities to Johnny Carson's green room; I was a great audience for his stories. One night we double-dated with my brother and his girlfriend, who spent the entire evening making a play for Ben. That was unusual; women were usually blindly in love with my brother.

I dated another guy I liked a lot. Lee, short and compact, ice blue eyes, liked me, too—but not a lot. I thought if I could make him jealous, he'd like me more. I decided to send seven roses (a dozen cost more than I was willing to spend) to myself the afternoon we would return to my apartment after a day at Jones Beach. I remember standing there, in the corner florist shop, surrounded by potted plants, trying to decide what to write on the card. I finally settled on: *Now am I forgiven, Southern Belle?* Lee would see the roses and the card, get jealous, go crazy over me. However, when the super in my building stopped us on our way in and handed me the roses, wilted after spending the day in the super's overheated room, no water, Lee's only comment was, "Who the fuck would send seven dead roses?" He never even saw the card.

———

Decades after my two years in New York City, while I was writing this book, I looked up the names that peopled that time. It was amazingly easy to find lost folks on social media. Natalie K. Noreen, Alejandro D'Antonio, Robert Bergman, Peter Griffith, Ted Shaw, Very British Married Man. Up popped their obituaries. I read the small print, stared at the old-person photographs. Yep, that's her. That's him, definitely. But, oh my gosh, how they'd aged before they died.

Very British Married Man left Ogilvy & Mather to serve in the UK Parliament. Ted Shaw, according to his obituary, was "an avid painter, photographer, dog lover." I never knew any of that about him. Peter Griffith ended up marrying five times. The actress, Dakota Johnson, is his granddaughter. The biggest shock was learning that Natalie K. Noreen and Alejandro D'Antonio got married not long after I left Filmex. Had they been a couple when I worked for them, when I made out in the cab with Alejandro? Is that why he didn't know my name when the three of us were back in the office the next morning?

# 9.

Meanwhile, I was serious about becoming a copywriter, so I took a night class at the New School, which hired the best copywriters and art directors in the city to teach their advertising classes. My instructor had been featured in *The New York Times.* My exotic New York life!

I assembled a portfolio of my work and registered with an employment agency that specialized in copywriting jobs in advertising. A super-hot ad agency brought me back for multiple interviews but, in the end, did not make an offer.

Benton & Bowles—not as creative an agency as Ogilvy & Mather, definitely not as creative as the agency that had turned me down, but good and solid—interviewed me several times. I met with the head of creative and the vice president and the president. The creative head gave me a test in which I had to invent two new products and create ad campaigns for them. I came up with a Kool-Aid–type drink in tea bags for kids. And a no-alarm alarm clock that woke you with a voice of your choosing—your mother's voice ("Wake up, sweetie! Breakfast is ready!"), your lover's voice ("Wake up, you sexy thing!")—whatever voice you wanted to hear first thing in the morning.

Benton & Bowles hired two of us young, female copywriters at the same time. The president told me he was betting on me to "surface first" (his words) and the vice president was "betting on the other gal." You might think having the president on my side was an asset, but, in fact, the news was disappointing. The vice president was young and gorgeous; I can still see his heavy-lidded eyes and dimpled chin. The president was old and blocky, heavy jaws. I was impressionable. I was romantic. I was immature.

I had my own office, which was really just a cubicle; I had a secretary named Hyacinth; and I had my own account, Vick's Formula 44 Cough Syrup. Before I wrote my first print ads and TV commercials, I ran a focus group to hear what people had to say about coughing—when they coughed and what they took to stop their coughs. I remember one heavyset man saying he always coughed after sex.

A half wall separated my cubicle from the next cubicle. My neighbor was an art director, a tall, bony, funny guy from Liverpool. Rutty skin. He'd probably had acne when he was a teenager. The wall between us came up as high as his neck. Glass ran along the top, up to his nose. He drew dozens of little sketches of mouths and moustaches and taped them all along the glass. He would stand there, resting his nose above one drawing, then another, so that he appeared to have thin lips and a little pencil moustache. Or full lips and a bristly moustache. Or a walrus moustache and a missing front tooth. On and on along the glass. He would just stand there, wearing his new face, waiting for me to look up from my typewriter and notice. I practically fell off my chair laughing every time.

My two years in the city were exactly what I needed to grow up and become independent, unmonitored by my southernness or anything else in me that might be suspicious of the altogether new.

Oh, those clear, bright fall mornings, snowy winter mornings, rainy spring mornings, sticky summer mornings I walked to work from my apartment on East 70th Street between First and Second Avenue—five crosstown blocks to Fifth Avenue, down to 53rd Street, to 666 Fifth Avenue, where Benton & Bowles occupied several floors. I loved my route to work; it felt like I owned those sidewalks. The fragrance of the streets, the city lavish with the exhaust of cars, cabs, and buses. I passed by construction workers who stopped their jackhammering to call out to me or wolf-whistle. I always waved back.

I'm not exaggerating when I say my life felt like an exhilaration. A sublime little world. A story truly my own. My amazing job—I not only got paid for doing something I'd been doing my whole life (writing); I got paid to hang out with creative people. My best friend lived two streets over, on 72nd. She worked at Etcetera Films, then the newly created *Ms.* magazine. We used to joke that our lives felt like we were starring in a TV show. I was discovering Central Park, artichokes, ski trips to Sugarbush, summer weekends at Fire Island, the Fifth Avenue bus, getting groped in a rush-hour subway, off-Broadway, Nancy Wilson in Harlem, The Beatles at Shea Stadium—the subway out to Flushing Meadows raucous with fans. I was aware of feeling lucky, grateful. Everything—every single thing—was fooling with my heart.

———

The same spirit of wonder I felt during my years in new and exotic New York City I unexpectedly feel in new and exotic old age—each a world any of us might be cowed by.

I'm often told, "You look young for your age." I am shameless in telling people how old I am, just so I'll get that reaction. I try to work my age into every conversation. In fact, after I say I'm eighty, I wait—seconds tick by—to give the other person a chance to tell me I don't look eighty.

Older women are invisible. Maybe setting people up to say how young I look is a way for me to avoid being relegated to the category of the unseen (or the not noticed). I don't own the sidewalks any more. Construction workers don't whistle. Young people rush by as I half stride along.

When we're young, we don't give old age a thought. And then, once we're firmly in this period of powering down, we're shocked to be here. Really, though, regardless of the number of candles on our cake, aren't we always shocked to be the age we are? The oldest we've ever been?

Old age = my move to New York City.

Each, a new, uncharted territory that cracks your brittle shell open and leaves you undefended. Each, a genesis story that brings with it the fear of the unfamiliar, as well as the exhilaration of trying out a new of kind of existence. You feel everything.

Old age's fear of the unfamiliar:

Just the other night, hours after I'd sautéed boneless chicken thighs, roasted Yukon Gold potatoes, and dressed a salad, hours after I'd delivered our plates to our two wooden TV tables and Henry and I ate, watching for the hundredth time *When Harry Met Sally,* I carried our empty plates back into the kitchen and saw that I'd left the burner on. Left the gas burner on! All that time! Could not believe I'd slid the chicken out of the frying pan onto our plates and then just walked away. I'd never done anything like that in my life! The blue flame was making a little noise that sounded like it was whispering, *tsk, tsk.*

Old age's exhilaration of trying out a new kind of existence:

I love the luxury of lying on the loveseat in my condo, sock feet propped up on a flat pillow, spending the afternoon reading. Not doing a thing but reading. Feels almost fugitive. I never would have spent so much time accomplishing nothing when I was younger.

I love deciding at five o'clock that I don't want to cook dinner, and Henry and I each fix our own bowl of cold cereal.

I love resolving to meditate on a regular basis, but then, day after day, forgetting. No feeling of guilt. Failure to do what I'd planned to do is no failure at all.

I love when someone calls and asks me to do something, and I say no. Just because I don't want to.

No doubt about it, the unfamiliarity of old age can be a fertile place. The privilege of aliveness. The freedom to create. The wonder of working out how this tapering slice of life will go, realizing there's not just one single correct way to do it.

We don't see the perks until we take the leap. Someone might promise to go with us, but then they back out. A friend can just up and get married. A brother can fly to France. A spouse can die. But even if a friend goes with us, even if a brother is a block away, even with a spouse beside us, we go alone, alone with ourselves. We go where it's not secure. We walk new streets. We learn a whole new language. We move through, one tiny moment and the next tiny moment. Through the weather. Through change. Until: *We are here*. This place where we've been set down. This place so full of possibilities.

# 10.

'm wondering how Henry sees aging, eighty-two-year-old Henry, the man I've spent most of my life with. In some ways, he's the same as when we met on that blind date so many years ago. In others— here we are, this last sliver of our life together—he's different.

In 1982, we took thirteen-year-old Laurie and ten-year-old Mike to Israel for Laurie's bat mitzvah. It was the only time our family had ever traveled with a tour group, which (because tensions were extraordinarily high in the Middle East that summer) was safer than going on our own. One day, all of us, in hushed clusters, were stepping gingerly along a twisting, wooded path, heading to the checkpoint between Israel and Lebanon. We would cross over into Lebanon, spend the day, meet Lebanese families in someone's home. Families meeting. Briefly. But still, meeting.

When we arrived at the checkpoint, we encountered young military men, rifles slung across their chests. Israelis on one side, Lebanese on the other. They were all *so* young, handsome. They smiled warmly at us, posed for our pictures.

We'd been warned though. Stay with the group.

But where was Henry?

Not with the group. Not anywhere in sight.

Our guide was frantic. Someone missing! "No, no!" he was muttering under his breath. He seemed to be darting off in ten different directions at once. We were darting off, too, all of us, back up the path, searching. I told myself Henry was fine, somewhere close by. But I could feel my pulse pumping in my ears.

And then!

Henry!

He'd stopped to fix a broken handrail.

He was crouched down, balancing on his heels, the gnarled wood railing across his broad shoulder. With his Swiss Army Knife, he was deepening the notch in the baluster. He would then reattach the railing, and all would be good.

What this said about my husband: If there was something wrong, he fixed it. It also said that whatever was passing in front of his face, that's what was important to him. Where he'd just been: unimportant. What lay ahead: unimportant. He was a person who was present, in the moment.

Henry and I don't travel any more. Not just the two of us, not with a group. Not by plane. Certainly not abroad. And I don't drive on the interstate. So, not by car. If Henry spotted a broken railing, he would not be agile enough to fix it. His spontaneity? Being in the moment? Like all of us old people, his mind is often in the past, reinhabiting that long-ago trip to Israel, other trips, experiences he and I have had, our family's experiences, his childhood, memories.

————

On a warmish Sunday afternoon in October 2021, I sit down next to him in our TV room/my office to ask for his thoughts on aging.

"Well, first of all, I never thought I would be this old!" he says. We're side by side on the khaki-colored, quilted sofa that traveled with us from our home on Scotland Avenue. The sofa cushions are as shapeless as you'd expect forty-year-old sofa cushions to be. Henry is about to watch some game—football? basketball? baseball? what sports season are we in?—when he starts talking. "I've outlived my mother by eleven years and my father by twenty. When I read obituaries, I see that most of the people who are dying were born in the 1930s, so I'm aware I don't have much time left. It's interesting...I feel so good at this point. I sort of wonder what is going to be the disease that finally takes me."

He reaches for the remote to turn on the TV. I can tell he's thinking, *How long has the game been on and I'm just now tuning in?* But then he decides to say more. He holds the remote, without clicking.

"My greatest sadness about dying is that I won't have you, our children, and our grandchildren anymore. I don't think we go any further than this. We're done. We don't meet up in heaven to be a unit again. You and I will be finished. Thank God, I went through this life with a woman like you as my partner. And with Laurie and Bob, Mike and Brooke being who they are. And with Lucy, Zoe, Tess, and Benjamin. Essentially, I'm a fortunate man having this be my lot in life."

# 11.

I decide to branch out and ask various friends how they view aging.

Judy, seventy-eight, and I have been close since we met in the kiddie pool with our youngest children—my Mike and her son, who's now married and a chef in Houston. Judy is warm and vivacious. She very aptly owned a party store for years, then worked in sales, and is now retired. She's divorced; her ex-husband died young. Her older son, married with one child, died suddenly in 2018.

Judy says, "I have positive feelings more than negative. The negative feelings are all about the physical aspects of getting older. I look in the mirror in the morning, when I'm brushing my teeth, and my hair looks like Harpo Marx and there are all these lines in my face—and I see my mother!"

We're on the phone, a gray, drizzly Saturday morning, a great morning to talk about the not-so-great parts of getting older.

She goes on, "The aging skin, the fallen boobs, the elasticity differences are very negative to me. Really, that's why I started playing pickleball. It's the last thing left for me. The last youthful thing left."

Now, a different tone in her voice: "The rest is positive, and the positive overrides the other. Sundays I don't dread anymore because I don't have to get ready for work the next day. Another thing I love about being older is that I know where I am in the scope of life, from the beginning to where I am now. I see the piece that's left. I know I've lived most of my life."

———

The day after Thanksgiving is also a good time to think about aging and our gratitude or lack of gratitude for it. My friend since first grade, Nancy Jan texts me her thoughts. She's eighty, married to her high school sweetheart, Billy, also my longtime friend. They live on the marsh in St. Simons Island, Georgia, and have two married children and five grandchildren. Nancy Jan was, hands down, the most popular girl in our class. In third grade, when boys went hunting with their dads, they brought her back dead rabbits.

Nancy Jan says, "As I grow older, I realize that my physical appearance is fading away. Since I've been a model and owned a modeling agency, I am probably more aware of this than other women. Sometimes I feel as though I'm invisible. But when I became eighty, I quit worrying about it. I do the best I can with what I got! Of course, there are things I can't do as well as before . . . simply because of aging . . . driving at night, getting in and out of the tub, remembering people's names, and, definitely, not hearing as well. Since my husband was diagnosed with cancer, I think more about death and dying. However, I'm not afraid to die. Because of my faith, I have the assurance that I will go to heaven and live eternally with Jesus when I die. This gives me great peace."

Nancy Jan's husband, Billy, died from bladder cancer not long after this.

———

It's the afternoon of New Year's Eve, and I call Betsy, eighty, who has been my friend since nursery school and who married her high school sweetheart. Hugh (also my friend since nursery school) died in the hospital in 2020, not of Covid, but during the first surge when hospital patients were not allowed to have visitors. The nurses allowed Betsy in to say goodbye. They did not allow their children in. Betsy, winsome and sparky, owned a gift shop in Rock Hill for years, filled with the antique clocks Hugh restored. She sold her store and is now a talented potter. She has three grown children and four grandchildren.

She says, "I don't really think that much about aging... until I look in the mirror! I look at my throat! I look at my chin! My knobby knuckles! Oh my gosh! Other than that, everything is pretty copacetic. And then I do something stupid on my cell phone and Sister says, 'Look up at the top, Betsy, and see that other people are included in the email. Hit Reply All! Not just Reply!' "

———

It's been a couple of weeks since our Breakfast Group discussed aging. The five of us are sitting in Dannye's sunporch, her fiddle-leaf fig not acting like a fiddle-leaf fig, cloaking one wide window and the ceiling in green.

I mention how interesting it is, getting my friends' views on growing older. Which starts the whole thing again. This time, about looks.

Trisha is on a totally different path now. "It's so damned shallow of me, but I just don't like looking old! My mother didn't care. It never occurred to her what she looked like as she aged."

Nobody asks what happened to the Trisha who declared two weeks ago she does not think about aging, ever. We're fine with strong statements that don't stand. Sometimes it's a change of heart. Sometimes it's a matter of not being in touch with ourselves. It's so hard to take a good, long, honest look at ourselves, especially if we don't like what we see.

Dannye asks, "Don't you think most people do not like their looks changing so much as they age?"

"I don't know," Trisha says. "It's just really shallow, but there's a reason I've had so much work done! There's a reason I still get Botox!"

Bobbie says, "Trisha, I think a lot about how I look."

Bobbie then tells how she recently drove out to Sharon Towers to check on the apartment she'll move into when the building is completed. "Oh my gosh, I saw this woman in the lobby. She looked so old. But then I thought, maybe we're the same age. And then I thought, do I look as bad as she looks?"

"Well," Dannye says, fluffing her white hair with one hand, "I'll never get over not having brown hair."

Dannye, Bobbie, and I colored our hair for years. No longer. Laurie J. and Trisha still color theirs. Both are blondes.

Now Dannye is holding up her left arm and, with the fingers of her right hand, jiggling her upper arm. "And I really don't like my arms."

———

Is it good to look young? Not good to look old?

What is it that makes me seek out that presumed compliment: "You look young for your age"?

I have an ambiguous relationship with my looks anyway. I grew up with a beautiful mother, though I was not thought of as beautiful. Of course, I would've liked to be beautiful, too, but feature for feature, our looks were quite different. Her expressive brown eyes, my droopy-lidded green ones. Her heart-shaped face, my long, narrow face. Her smile, my solemn expression; when I was little, people were always telling me to smile. Oddly, people were also always telling me I looked just like my mother. I don't think they were seeing straight. They knew how alike our personalities and temperaments were, how we seemed to share an unnamable quality, the way we moved or talked or thought, and they just assumed our alikeness included our looks. I loved being the daughter of a beautiful woman. I believe Brenda felt the same way. After all, Mother belonged to us. She was ours. Which made us special, in a tangential way.

Even when Brenda went through her early years being beautiful—her cherubic Shirley Temple face and mass of Shirley Temple curls—I was okay with it. When she was seven and I was four, she was chosen to be flower girl at Winthrop College's May Day celebration. I loved her pink net gown with the bows dotting the skirt, the tiny white flowers in her hair, even the attention she received. The beginning of the afternoon, when people told her how pretty she was, she smiled, messed a little with her hair, and said, "Thank you." By the end of the afternoon, she was smiling and saying, "I know."

"You look young for your age, Judy."

"Thank you."

"You look young for your age, Judy."

"Thank you."

"You look young for your age, Judy."

"I know."

But Brenda didn't end up beautiful. It's not that she was *unat-tractive* (and neither am I). She was tall and slender, and her skin, because she did not believe in sunbathing, was smooth and creamy. But, really, our looks—ordinary. Maybe the fact that we shared this status made it okay for both of us. I'm not sure how it would've felt to either of us to go through a life with a beautiful mother *and* a beautiful sister.

Sunday mornings, growing up, Brenda and I spread the "Weddings and Engagements" section of *The Charlotte Observer* across the hooked rug in the den on Eden Terrace—all those inky pages of brides and fiancées. We lay side by side on our stomachs. Then one of us would say: "1-2-3 pick!" We would each point to the one—*the one*—the prettiest, the woman we longed to be. If Brenda's beauty-seeking forefinger and mine landed on the same flawless face, whoever arrived first "got her" and the other had to go with second choice. Over and over—1-2-3 pick!—until the prettiest brides and fiancées had all been chosen. Sacredly serious business, those rankings. Before breakfast. Still in our pajamas and bedroom slippers. We took care of this before we did another thing, mapped each face, scrutinized pageboys and bangs and pixie cuts, blonds, and brunettes. How deeply we cared about beauty. But we didn't know why. Didn't understand where beauty belonged when it came to judging worth.

The earliest Miss America Brenda and I rhapsodized over was Bess Myerson, crowned in 1945. I was four. Brenda, seven. It was rumored Bess Myerson was Jewish, which we thought made her practically related to us. Those days, in Rock Hill, most Jewish people we knew *were* relatives. Our other favorite Miss America was Marian McKnight. Hometown: Manning, South Carolina. Our very own state! Practically next door! All that alliteration! Those M's! Marian McKnight from Manning. Miss America, 1957. Brenda and I were so thrilled, so proud, you'd think she lived next door.

Was it a small-town thing? The way people who live in small towns can be even more hierarchical than big-city dwellers? How we search for systems to gauge a person's merit? Look for a reference point? Was it a southern thing? Life so languid we had nothing better to do? Or was it just something girls cared about in the 1940s and '50s? What made *who is beautiful* such a pressing issue? And who set the narrow standards? Growing up with a mother everyone said was beautiful—even though I always claimed it a plus, not a minus— can tinker with your vision and priorities. It can dictate what you're magnetically drawn to, what excites your inner eye. Maybe it does all sorts of things to a girl.

Truth is, I was surrounded by beauty, not just in my home, but also close to home. I had the same beautiful friends from nursery school through high school graduation (and to this day). Betsy was Miss W. T. S. (Miss Winthrop Training School was always the prettiest girl in the senior class.) She was also voted "Most Attractive." Nancy Jan was homecoming queen and head cheerleader. Kathryne was May Queen and Miss Hi Miss.

I was editor of the school newspaper, third honor graduate, voted "Best All-Round" and "Most Versatile." (I recently told all this to a friend from high school, and she said, "But, Judy, you need to say you were a cheerleader." Okay. Add that.) I'm not complaining about the type of recognition I received as a teenager. But you can't help but notice certain things.

I want to be sure I'm being clear-eyed and honest here. I don't believe I have ever resented my friends or my mother. I thought being solidly in their circle upped my value. If these girls are my friends and this woman is my mother, then I must belong right up there in their hallowed league.

It would be an interesting study—nonbeautiful daughters of beautiful mothers, nonbeautiful friends of beautiful girls. If it's a teenager you're studying, you're looking at someone at an age when her self-confidence can be crushed with a glance, or the lack of a glance. What are our true feelings, those of us who are sidekicks to grace?

Is there, deep down, the sharp edge of jealousy?

Or a whole lot of admiration?

Or both?

When I think of the beauty I was surrounded by, the image I get is me curling in close to them. I knew them. I knew their beauty was not just on the outside. It permeated their every cell. And I was linked to them. If not beautiful myself, then I was, at least, adjacent.

But context is everything. And even though this might not speak well of me, being surrounded by all that beauty must have created something that closed me off—or granted me the right to close others off—in ways I hardly knew. This preoccupation with beauty pulled on me, punctuated my life. I defined others by it. Defined myself by it. And yes, wanted it. No begrudging in that wanting. No resenting. Just wanting.

———

After my day at Kenneth in New York, I actually relished looking at myself in the mirror, even in the strong light of morning. I not only thought I had matured into an attractive-enough young woman, I'd also learned, thanks to Mr. Kenneth, how to make the most of my looks. I stood at the bathroom mirror in my apartment before leaving for work and studied my eyes, the fringe of false lashes, the taupe and alabaster shadow on my lids. I studied my brown hair, streaked with blond. Sometimes I wore what was called a fall, which

I'd bought at Macy's one hurried lunchtime; I'd left the office with short hair, returned with hair so long and thick I could bat it with one casual hand. When I checked myself in the full-length mirror on the back of my bedroom door, my legs looked really good—my short skirt and three-inch heels.

Vanity. For the first time in my life.

It felt great.

You might say—near the end of my second year in New York, around the time I met Henry—I was my very prettiest.

And yet.

I didn't meet Henry's parents until our wedding weekend. Granted, we became engaged on our third date. And we married a short two months later. But I can't understand why his parents didn't fly up from Miami that summer to meet their son's fiancée or why we didn't fly down.

The afternoon before our wedding, Henry and his mom were driving around Charlotte in his Volkswagen, running errands. She and Henry's dad had arrived the night before, which is when we'd met. We'd all had dinner at Henry's sister Ruth's house, where his parents were staying. I have no recollection of that dinner, just that I finally met my in-laws-to-be.

Now, Henry and his mom were shoulder to shoulder in his Volks-wagen, that tight little car, stick shift between them, his burly self, her tiny, four-eleven, barely one-hundred-pound self. They were chatting about his new life in Charlotte, about the office he would soon open, when she grabbed his arm, those Revlon red fingernails, and said, "You know, Henry, it's not too late to call off the wedding."

"Mom! What are you saying?" He nearly ran off the road.

"Well, you've just moved and you're starting a practice and you don't know Judy very well. And, anyway, she's not that pretty."

A quick swerve, and Henry *did* pull off the road, bumping up to the curb.

"I can't believe you said that!" he yelled, his face inches from hers. "Judy is *beautiful*! And I love her! And we're getting married *tomorrow*!"

Not that pretty.

Not that pretty.

When I was actually my prettiest.

Henry didn't tell me about that conversation until long after his mother had died. Imagine poor Henry, all that time, wanting to tell me but not wanting me to know. Why would he want to tell me? We've always been a couple who talk freely with one another. Keeping this from me felt like a burden to him. But what words would he use?

Surprisingly, his mom and I, not long after the wedding, developed a close relationship, albeit a relationship with some not-so-close moments here and there. But that was her way with every family member. I was the one—not her daughter, Ruth, with whom she'd had a tiff—who took care of her when lung cancer was bringing her life to an end.

————

It's been fifty-three years since Henry's and my wedding weekend. You can clearly see the marks of time and experience on my face. The lines make me look like a linen blouse that should've been ironed better. I'm not crazy about looking in the mirror. The only photograph of myself I can stand is on my new driver's license, but then I always like my driver's license pictures, my face obscured by the superimposed columns of the state capitol building. I joke that maybe I should order ten wallet-sized prints from the DMV to give to friends.

Also, there are my leg veins.

And the saggy skin holding each knee in place.

That space between my waist and breasts, thick like a shelf. Used to be my thinnest body part. My waist was so small. My very tiny cousin, Debbie, who's more my sister than my cousin, tells me, "Oh my God, Judy, I've got that, too! Where did it come from?"

All the definitions of my body softened.

And is that a hump on my back? I twist to check it out in the mirror, but I can't tell for sure.

My perfect teeth, not perfect now. People used to ask if I wore braces when I was young. No, my teeth just happened to be very straight. Now all my teeth are trying to be my front teeth. Pushing forward in my small mouth.

And how many chins do I have? Lord, I've turned into Uncle Albert, my father's older brother.

And the basal cell carcinomas the dermatologist keeps finding. I hate he's so careful.

My arms. Oh, my arms. When I lie in bed, holding my book up to the light, my arm looks like a deflated balloon. I can't be sure it's really *my* arm. As though someone slipped in and unscrewed my thin, young arm and inserted this thing.

All the body changes distilled and concentrated here at the end.

———

Here's what growing old is like:

Henry kept his 1964 beige Volkswagen Beetle for years after we were married. How he loved that car, loved to tell what he'd paid for it: $1500, brand new. He bought it with money he'd earned when he was a student at the Illinois College of Optometry, working summers as a bus driver in Chicago. But when his mother learned he'd bought a German car, she was beside herself. Shocked. Furious. World War II too recent. Henry's father's cousins, who'd escaped from the Nazis by hiding in an Austrian forest, too dear.

The last months of that car's life, early 1972, Henry would park in our driveway, walk into the kitchen of our duplex while I was fixing dinner, and tell me which part fell off on his way home.

"Well, today, the front bumper dropped off in the middle of the street. I nearly ran over it."

"You'll never guess what happened. When I went to open the glove compartment, the whole outside cover just fell off in my hand."

"Taillight out. I don't mean the bulb needs replacing. I mean, the entire taillight is gone. I guess it's somewhere between the office and here."

Little by little, that car gave in. There was nothing more to it.

Just like us. Part by part. Change after (unwelcome) change.

Except for.

My hair.

My crown of white, white hair.

How many times a week does someone tell me, "Your hair is beautiful!"

Thank you.

Thank you.

I know.

The color is everything. Incandescent. Luminous. A miracle of white. Like snow. The same shade as my mother's.

It's difficult to locate the points on a map of my life when I was not okay with my looks, then when I was okay with my looks, then when I was not okay again. What are looks all about anyway? What do changes in our appearance even mean? Maybe they're just life's little accidents.

# 12.

Here's Darnell, sixty-six, my sensitive friend whose feelings are always appealingly just beneath the surface, my creative friend who's a poet and fiction writer. It wasn't until after she became a grandmother that her first book was published. Darnell met her second husband, William, on an online dating site. She was doing research for a short story she was writing about a woman who answered a personal ad, and she came across William's ad. They were married in 2000. He died in 2020. Darnell had married her first husband at eighteen, birthed a son at nineteen (who himself is now married with three daughters), a daughter at twenty-one (now married with a stepson). Darnell is raising William's great-grandson, seven-year-old Bryson (whom she and William took in at age three, adopted at age five).

"It's sad thinking of all the things you can no longer do. For example, I can't hop any more. When you're raising a seven-year-old great-grandson, you notice that. So...hopping is out! You know, my life changes every twenty years. After my divorce, I raised two children as a single parent. That's about twenty years. Then William and I were married twenty years. Now I wonder, how will the last twenty go? I'm the age my father was when he died. I hope I have my mother's genes. She lived to eighty-five. I just want to live long enough to see Bryson graduate from college."

———

My last grandparent died when I was nine years old. I had only seen my grandfather—my mother's father—a few times during his life; Grandpa Bogen lived in Florida and was not very interested in visiting his children and grandchildren. After my parents died, I found a postcard from Grandpa Bogen to my mother, his reckless handwriting: *Sorry I haven't written. Been busy getting married again.*

I remember, during one of his rare visits to Eden Terrace, his pacing, from our front hall through the den to the French doors in the living room and back again. Sometimes he'd let little farts go. Or maybe it was his shoes squeaking. He wore an elk's tooth on a short gold chain hooked to his vest. I wanted to touch that elk's tooth, wanted to know if it was as smooth as it looked and if the point was sharp. I never summoned the courage to ask. I don't believe I ever saw him not wearing a three-piece suit and not smoking a cigar. He called me *Flimely*, Yiddish for "little bird." An okay nickname; I *was* small. And at least he saw me, even if he didn't talk to me much.

Grandpa Bogen traveled to Rock Hill from Miami on a bus. But instead of my mother picking him up at the Greyhound station and bringing him to the house, he would not tell her when he was arriving. Instead, he would walk right over to the Elks Club, a short distance from the station, and play gin rummy in the illegal poker room upstairs, late into the night. His true love: gambling. Finally, at some ungodly hour, he'd call Mother: "I'm here!"—as though he'd just stepped down from the bus and could hardly wait to see us. I remember overhearing my parents' whispers into the night, fragments—Mother's hurt feelings, my father referring to his father-in-law as *that rascal.*

I have few memories of the other grandparent who was alive after I was born, Grandma Kurtz, my father's mother. Well, really, my only memory is that she was stout and diabetic. I loved the little glass insulin bottles she unpacked from her suitcase when she arrived from Atlanta, loved that I was the one she gave them to after she'd injected her fleshy arm or thigh. I was the only kid in the neighborhood with an insulin bottle collection. She died when I was seven.

I was so envious of my friends when their grandparents came for a stay or took them on trips to the beach, their gentle stories of those soft, old people. Once, I happened to be at my friend's house when her grandmother was visiting. It was the first time I'd met the grandmother, but I pressed up against that thin, old woman, so that there was nothing for her to do but drape her shaky arm around my shoulder. I asked if I could adopt her for my grandmother. I watched her mouth widen into a smile. "Of course, sweetie," she cooed. "Of course."

I thought, *Ahh. Now I have a grandparent.*

I never saw her again.

She lived a nice, long life; I just never happened to be there when she came.

Like me, Laurie and Mike lost their grandparents when they were young. Henry's father died at sixty-one; Laurie was two, and Mike wasn't born yet. I have to laugh when I think how Henry and I believed Laurie was old enough to remember Papa Moe. He was so affectionate, and that thick, straight, white hair; how could she forget him? The other three grandparents—Henry's mother and both my parents—all died at seventy-one, within two years of each other. Laurie was eleven when her last grandparent (my mother) died; Mike was eight. All four grandparents had been involved and loving, but their involvement and love was cut short.

Henry's mom, after she moved from Miami to Charlotte, brought Laurie and Mike strawberries and grapes when they were sick. Laurie, at ages eight, nine, and ten, always became homesick when she tried to spend the night with a friend. We could count on her soggy phone call around eleven—*Come get me!* Henry's mom was determined to help her pull off a whole night. Laurie and her Big Bird sleeping bag arrived at Nanny's apartment, she and Nanny both feeling confident this sleepover would be "the one." And it was. Laurie slept soundly in Nanny's bed. Nanny spent the night in Laurie's sleeping bag on the floor beside the bed.

My mother sat cross-legged on her living room floor with Laurie and Mike, building intricate card houses. They used so many decks of cards, their houses looked like shopping malls, those flat-roofed buildings spread across the carpet. And always, they went to Sky City on the bypass, where Laurie and Mike could stroll up and down the aisles, loading a shopping cart with toys.

My father taught Mike how to read the baseball stats in the newspaper. When Mother had Alzheimer's and was in a nursing home in Charlotte, my father left their home in Rock Hill and lived with us, then with Brenda and her family, back and forth between our two houses, so that he could spend all day, every day, at Mother's bedside. Each morning at breakfast, he and Mike crouched over the sports pages, analyzing the box scores from the previous day's games: who got walked, who got hits, who scored. The pros and cons of each player.

"Who do you like best, Granddaddy?" Mike would ask, his face turned up to his grandfather's face. "Pete Rose or Reggie Jackson?"

My father would think long and hard before he answered. The two of them took all this very seriously.

Years later, at a family wedding, I was standing in the buffet line with my cousin Jack, eighteen years older than me, son of my father's older brother, Easy. I asked him to tell me about our grandfather, my father's father (and, of course, Jack's father's father), whom Jack had known well.

"Tell me anything, whatever occurs to you," I said. "All I've ever heard about our grandfather is that he was a scholar. I don't even understand what that means. Maybe he was a studious man, but he was a shopkeeper! Tell me something real."

My cousin thought for a minute, then said, "Well, he really knew baseball stats. He could recite them for hours."

I love how certain traits or passions or whatever you call them burrow down through generations in a family.

I *don't* love how a lack of grandparents burrows down through generations in a family. Where there should be genesis stories of grandchildren on grandparents' laps, there are gaps.

So then, another theme running through my family: Where are the grandparents?

———

Mike's first Grandparents Day at school, when he was in kindergarten, my father was the only grandparent able to attend, and he fulfilled that duty with joy. Mother was in the nursing home, and both of Henry's parents had died. My father and Mike were so animated telling me about their day; they even joked back and forth about the plaid sport coat another grandfather had worn. *He was wearing his sofa!* The next year, my father was no longer alive. Still, whether these first graders had grandparents or not, they were required to write a Grandparents Day invitation letter. I can just picture Mike at his desk, too shy to ask his teacher what to do, stewing over whose name should go after "Dear . . ."

———

Mike and Laurie are not the only children in this world to grow up without grandparents. Just as I'm not the only one.

However, I may be one of the few who, beginning in childhood, could hardly wait to become a grandparent. I was not only curious about it, I aspired to it. Lots of little girls dream of becoming a mother when they are older. They imagine what it would be like to hold their very own baby, a spongy cheek nuzzled into their neck. Not many spend their growing up years setting their sights on a spongy cheek nuzzling into their *aging* neck. My friends played mama with their dolls. I played grandma with mine. I even made my voice quivery to sound old when I sang to the rubbery baby I cradled.

Is it any wonder I have an almost religious commitment to being a grandmother? Why I do it in overdrive?

———

Every August since the early 1980s, Henry and I have rented a house and taken our family to the beach for a week. Early on, it was the four of us—Henry and me, Laurie and Mike. Later, one or both of the kids brought a friend. Then Mike and Brooke became engaged, and she joined us. Then Laurie and Bob became engaged, and he joined us. Laurie and Bob then brought their identical twin daughters, Lucy and Zoe. Mike and Brooke brought their daughter, Tess. Then their son, Benjamin.

A highlight of our beach week is a birthday dinner for Henry, even though his actual day isn't until after we get home.

Summer of 2021, late afternoon, everyone was preparing for the big event. The grandchildren—Lucy and Zoe, eighteen; Tess, sixteen; Benjamin, thirteen—were busy twirling crepe paper streamers and tying balloons to every stationary thing in the dining area. Tess was the chief architect; she always has a vision of how a decorated room should look. She started decorating before her brother and cousins joined in, and she was still decorating after they'd wandered off. She had made place cards with her artistic, swirled calligraphy; she usually positioned herself next to me. Lucy and Zoe took turns sitting on the other side of me; Benjamin popped up in different spots.

Laurie and Brooke were in the kitchen, frying and chopping, putting together their annual fish taco feast. Since we had all changed out of our wet bathing suits and combed our hair, we decided to snap our annual family photo out on the beach, before dinner. This usually ends up taking a long time. Laurie sets up the tripod; Benjamin clowns around; everyone kids Benjamin (the burden of being the only male grandchild *and* the youngest); Mike and Bob kid each other, how they don't want to stand anywhere near the other; we settle in for the shot. Laurie runs to get in the picture just before the click.

When the photo shoot was over, the rest of the family raced back across the beach, up the steep steps onto the long, splintery dock, through the screened porch, inside the house. Mike hung back with Henry and me, helping Henry navigate the deep sand with his cane. We went slow. But Mike was the slowest of us three. In fact, he seemed to pause every few seconds, which didn't make sense. Mike is strong and fit; he's one of those people who actually enjoys working out. But here he was, slow, slow.

When we finally reached the screened porch, the others jumped out, wearing party hats, blowing those little striped noisemakers, yelling, "Happy birthday!"

Oh, that's why Mike was taking his sweet time. He was giving the rest of the family a chance to get ready.

But, wait. They weren't looking at Henry. They were looking at me. My first impulse was to say, "No, no! You've got it wrong! It's Pop's birthday! Mine's not till October!"

They were clearly making me the star of this celebration.

Since this was a big birthday for me—my eightieth—they wanted to make it special. How better to make it special than to celebrate at the beach? I had already told them I didn't want a party; I just wanted to be with family.

Laurie had asked me, while we were out on the beach that afternoon, to name my favorite records from the 1950s. I thought she was just indulging me. So, I let her indulge me. "Good Night, Sweetheart," the song that ended all our high school dances. Oh, and "Earth Angel"—very romantic. I was filling in little memories attached to each song. Elvis's "Don't Be Cruel." Any of Elvis's early songs. "Money Honey"—great to dance to. "Sixty-Minute Man," also great to dance to. My cousin Debbie's mother would not let her buy "Sexy Ways," so she played my record at my house for hours. "Let the Good Times Roll." On and on I went. *I*, in fact, was on a roll. Laurie was finding the songs on her phone and playing bits for me. Sitting under the umbrella—family all around, some reading, Bob and the grandkids building a giant crab in the sand, shovels and buckets, waves breaking close by, the music I used to hear at The Pad in Ocean Drive, just an hour away from where I was now burying my toes deeper and deeper in the sand.

Once we were all back inside the house, ready for the birthday party, the songs from my teenage years were *wah-wah*ing from the speaker on the shelf between the kitchen and dining room.

The flour and corn tacos were soft and warm, the shrimp and little pillows of mahi mahi crispy. Guacamole, chopped tomatoes and purple cabbage and lettuce and jalapenos and cucumbers and mango salsa, chipotle mayo, enough toppings in little bowls to cover every inch of that long pine table. Two cakes—one from the grocery store and a chocolate lava cake Benjamin had made. Candles. Singing. Wishes. Presents. Homemade cards. Just a birthday party. An utterly ordinary scene. A family going about its life.

So much of life is, in fact, lived on a small scale. Yet, that evening felt enchanted. Shimmering.

I kept exclaiming how amazingly lucky I was to reach eighty. I could have wept from happiness over what I had—maybe also wept from sadness over what could be taken away. But that wasn't my thought then.

My thinking: *Imagine! I've lived long enough to hug my grandchildren.*

My grandparents were an absence in my life. My children's grandparents were an absence in their lives.

I'm present. Here. Now. All the layers of grandparenthood accruing.

———

In telling my stories, on the page and in life, I slide back and forth between then and now. Not so much talk of what's coming next. Of course, what's-coming-next is never guaranteed. But it's even less so at this age. I might wonder about the future, might make plans for the future, but I won't necessarily get a future. The main thing: I am lucky to make it this far. As I move toward the end, grandparenthood is a way to reattach myself to this world. I'm about to exit stage left, but look what's entering stage right. That's the beauty of grandparenthood. It's the future. It's what comes after us.

No wonder I rifle back through the stories about my grandchildren over the years, tell and retell those stories as though other people don't have their own to tell.

Maybe grandparenthood is my ultimate genesis story. It, of course, begins with a beginning. A brand-new life, a dimpled hand, squinty little eyes that, blink, blink, resist closing in sleep before finally giving in. A new generation. *Look! That valentine face! Just like my mother's! Remember Mother's valentine face?*

Growing older and becoming a grandparent dovetail. Growing older is what put me in position to be a grandmother. I get to have the second because of the first.

# 13.

That great shift in my life began on December 30, 2001, when Laurie and Bob, both thirty-two, spent the night with us on Scotland Avenue, on their way to the mountains for New Year's Eve with friends. Uncharacteristically, Bob had called that afternoon to ask if a visit would be okay, after dinner; might be late. Usually, Laurie would be the one to check with us about plans. *More important, I thought, why are they veering out of their way to Charlotte when they could drive straight from Durham to Linville?*

Laurie and Bob had been friends at Duke University. They started dating after college, when Laurie was living in New York City, working toward a graduate degree in graphic design at Parsons School of Design and waitressing at Banana Cafe. Bob, a Russian studies major at Duke, was living at home with his parents, working in a hardware store in Salisbury, Connecticut. They eventually moved in together in the Village, then moved to Durham, then got married. (They later moved to Charlotte, but I'm getting ahead of myself here.) Bob's work: computer programming. Laurie ran her own graphic design firm. She's the type of person who gets excited just greeting the day, that ebullient spirit. Adventure is evident in every part of her life. She's the kid who spent her junior year of high school with a French family in Rennes who spoke no English. She's the kid who spent a postcollege year teaching sailing at Club Med in Turks and Caicos. Bob is steady and steadfast, with a quick, smart wit. He's also bighearted. His smile is warm and friendly and shows front teeth with a slight separation, all part of his charm.

The four of us were in our kitchen on Scotland Avenue, Henry and Bob standing on one side of the island, their elbows resting on the countertop. Laurie and I sat on wooden stools on the other side. They'd just come in from the car. I had made chocolate chip cookies, and we were sliding the plate back and forth.

"Now," Laurie said, "we have a present for you. Dad, you sit. Here. On this stool." She gave him her stool. He and I were now side by side. "First, I have to take off my sweater though. I'm hot."

She was making a big deal of wrestling her sweater off, one arm, the other arm, all slow motion, sweater over the head, straighten out the sleeves, one, the other. Odd for this to be so problematic for her; she's quite agile. She ended up tousling her hair, which is reddish-brown and thick and curly and, really, looks tousled even when it's not.

She casually dropped the sweater on the counter and turned to face us. She was wearing a plain white T-shirt. I couldn't read her expression. She just stood there, letting us take in her T-shirt. Which I realized, as I focused, was not plain at all. The T-shirt, not her expression, was what she wanted us to read.

On the front, in her handwriting, were big, bold, black letters: #1 GRANDKID. With a no-nonsense arrow pointing down to her belly.

It is not an exaggeration to say, at that moment, the universe began spinning like a whirligig. I immediately slid off my stool and started jumping up and down, flapping my arms like a half-lost person, jumping, flapping, I could not stop, I swear to you, I just had to keep moving. It all felt totally involuntary. I had no say in what my body decided to do with itself. Henry was still on his stool, but laughing and shouting along with me. You couldn't understand what either of us was saying because we were making so much noise. Laurie and Bob just stood there, watching, like they were the parents and we were the kids.

Then we tumbled into each other, big, enveloping hugs. As though the four of us were taking the world into our arms.

"When is it due?" Henry finally asked, in an almost normal voice.

"September fourth or fifth. I'm four weeks and three days pregnant."

"Let's go in the den and talk," I said, *my* almost normal voice. "If I don't sit down, I'm going to fall down."

We practically tripped over each other, puppylike, leaving the kitchen and heading into the den.

Henry and I sat on the loveseat, Laurie and Bob on the sofa. The two of them were gathered in so close, they could have fit on a barstool.

"Okay. Now," I said, "tell us everything."

Laurie had stopped taking her birth control pills almost a year before. She described how, month after month, they had become more and more stressed. Bob corrected her, "Well, it wasn't stressful trying to have a baby. It was just stressful trying to have a baby."

"We get it," Henry and I both said, at the same time. Laughs all around.

They'd thought she might have been pregnant before our annual family beach trip the past August. "Wouldn't it have been something?" Laurie said. "To be able to tell y'all and Mike and Brooke together? But then I wasn't."

At Thanksgiving, they thought again she might be pregnant. She wasn't.

And then she was late. She put off taking the test. And put off taking the test. Until this morning, the next to the last morning of 2001. She peed on the stick and left it in the bathroom. She didn't want to watch the negative result appear. She emptied the dishwasher. Paid a bill in her office. Finally, she forced herself to return to the bathroom.

The extra stripe was there.

Positive.

No mistake about it.

She'd heard the extra stripe can appear but be faded and watery. *This* extra stripe was boldly pink.

The four of us talked into the night. What about names? Maybe Mollie for a girl, after Henry's mother. Or Benjamin for a boy, after my father. They also liked Griffin. (Griffin Smithwick?) No, they had not decided whether they wanted to know the baby's sex before it was born. Yes, she felt fine.

———

The next morning, over scrambled eggs, bacon, and grits, I told the dream I'd just had:

*I'm holding my granddaughter, who's about four months old. I'm making little noises, getting lots of smiles. When I look closer at her face, though, I see that it's not my granddaughter, after all. It's Laurie. She's wearing the bathing suit she really did wear at that age, the one with pink stripes (like the pregnancy test). Her little shape is so familiar to my hands—the curve of her head, the reddish hair, though not much of it then. Next—in that way that one image in a dream cuts cleanly to an-other image—it's my granddaughter again.*

How stitched together we all are. One to the next.

———

Henry did the breakfast dishes; I sat in the den with Laurie, and we talked while Bob showered. Then Laurie went up to shower, and Bob and I talked. I was like David Letterman, interviewing one guest after another.

Now they were ready to leave for the mountains. The four of us stood at the back door. Bob was holding their overnight bags. We hugged good-bye, said all the things you're imagining we said.

Laurie followed Bob to their car in the driveway. Before she opened her door, she turned toward Henry and me and said, "Oh, one more thing I want to discuss. What if everyone at the New Year's Eve party notices I'm not drinking? They'll know right away I'm pregnant."

Before either Henry or I could answer, she opened her door and added, "I'll just sip a beer. To keep them from suspecting."

"No! Don't take even one sip!" I blurted out, the volume on my anxiety dial many notches higher than I'd intended. "It's not worth it! Make up something!"

She was now climbing into the car, swinging her legs around, shutting her door. I'd either given her a great suggestion and she felt reassured. Or I'd given her way more than she was asking for and she was making her getaway.

But my reaction. My visceral reaction to that decision of hers to just sip a beer. I surprised myself with my counterblast. She'd been on her own for a lot of years. She was thirty-two. Surely, by now, I trusted her judgment. I have never been much of a drinker, but I didn't abstain from a glass of wine every now and then when I was pregnant. It wasn't taboo in those days, and our babies turned out fine. Why did I suddenly feel the need to reach out and grab hold of my daughter? Like the newspaper columnist Erma Bombeck writing about her daughter walking down the aisle at her wedding and Erma wanting to run after her: "Wait! I'm not finished with you yet!"

———

Every time I was close to falling asleep, six words popped up in blinking neon above my head: *I'm going to be a grandmother.* Then came the worries: *Will Laurie go snowboarding in February? Will she go to her friend's wedding in Hawaii the end of June—two months before she's due? When will they finish renovating the house?* (They'd bought a fixer-upper, a *real* fixer-upper, a 1923 bungalow, and they were doing the work themselves.) *Paint fumes? Pregnant woman on tall ladder? Is she eating right?*

The next day, I could hardly stand not talking about what would soon occur in our lives. Henry was at the kitchen table, reading the newspaper, eating his Grape-Nuts, bananas, blueberries, and strawberries. I walked over, very close, and said, "Let's talk about the baby."

"Okay." He folded the paper in half and pushed it aside. "Let's talk about the baby."

I sat down across from him and rehashed every detail of our evening with Laurie and Bob, what each of them said, what we said, what we did, what they did, everything. Henry acted as though he had not been there, had not actually experienced it all himself. As though, ever since last night, he'd been waiting to hear someone tell him what he already knew.

That satisfied me for the moment.

Until he was eating lunch. That's when I started "Let's talk about the baby" all over again. Throughout his ham and Swiss cheese sandwich.

Then I decided to just pace. From the kitchen through the den to our bedroom and back. Every time I skirted our bed and straightened Laurie's T-shirt (which she'd left) hanging on the brass knob of the window shutter, I was happy to see that arrow still pointing to the next generation.

# 14.

aurie and Bob's first ob-gyn appointment. Laurie's voice, when she called to report late that afternoon, was buoyant. (How we mothers live to hear that lilt in our children's voices.)

"Okay, the doctor rolls in the ultrasound," she was saying. I sat down at my built-in desk in the kitchen. My ears were cocked for the news, anticipating hearing that the baby's fine, all's well, here we go, imagine, a baby, on its way! I was smiling already, holding the phone in one hand and, with the other, writing down on a pad of paper what she said—*okay, the doctor rolls in the ultrasound*—so that I could tell Henry, who was playing racquetball at the Y and wouldn't get home until later. My pencil needed sharpening, but I sure wasn't going to interrupt to go find a pencil sharpener. Did we even own a pencil sharpener?

"I'm lying on the table," she was saying. "Bob is standing beside me, and the doctor says, 'You see the kidney-bean shape? That's your uterus. You see this tiny circle here, inside the uterus? That's your baby, and everything looks great. Now I'm going to show you something that's going to really freak you out.'"

I was still drawing the kidney bean, although it looked more like a string bean. I erased the bean and made it fatter and then drew the tiny circle inside. I wanted to be sure not to leave anything out when I told Henry. I was thinking he was lucky I'm such a good artist.

Laurie kept going: "Then the doctor points to a cloudy area and says, 'This is the yolk sac. That's what your baby is living off of until it implants. Now, see the tiny circle over here, also in the uterus? That's your other baby.'"

"Wait. *What?*" I threw down my pencil. The pad of paper fell to the floor.

"We're going to have twins!"

Twins? Twins?

I scraped my chair back over the hardwood floor and started jumping up and down and laughing and crying. I was totally alone. In my kitchen. Not another soul around. And I was jumping up and down, making a racket, like I'd turned plum loony! My scalp was so hot it felt cold.

Then Laurie and I were both talking at once.

"What did y'all *do* when she said that?" I managed to say over her.

"Well, I was lying down but Bob wasn't, so he fell on the floor. No, I'm joking! We both kept cracking up. For the rest of the visit. When we were checking out, I told the woman who was handling the financial stuff, 'I'm sorry we keep laughing, but we just found out we're having twins.' She then started laughing because she's a twin!"

"Did the doctor have anything else to say?"

"She said the babies are both the same size, 7.4 millimeters, which is about a quarter inch. That's something they look for, that both babies are growing at approximately the same rate."

In fact, the doctor wanted her back in two weeks. Both babies were feeding off the same yolk sac, and she wanted to be sure they pulled away and became self-sufficient. Sometimes one twin doesn't make it, and she wanted Laurie and Bob to be aware that this could happen.

Yes, they heard—or maybe Laurie said they saw—two heartbeats, two tiny flutterings.

"Oh, and Dr. Cole said she doesn't think we should go to Hawaii for Michelle's wedding in June. Too close to the time of delivery. Twins are full-term at thirty-six weeks, which would be the beginning of August."

"That takes care of one of my worries," I said. "Are you going snowboarding?"

"She said it's perfectly all right for us to go snowboarding in February. It has a lot to do with my ability."

I forged ahead. "Laurie, I know this has to be your decision, and I promise I'll be okay with whatever you decide. But would you mind if I tell you what I'm thinking?"

"Okay," she said. *Timing. It's everything. She was in a great mood, I could say anything.*

"I just feel like this is such a limited time, being pregnant. Why not take every precaution you can? You can be an expert snowboarder and still fall. Plus, you don't know how expert the skiers around you are. They could easily plow into you. I promise, every year after this, Dad and I will happily keep your . . . your babies! . . . and you and Bob can go snowboarding. Now, having said that, I know this is your decision. I just wanted to have my say so I won't feel later I should've spoken up. Is that all right?" *Did I push too far?*

"It's fine."

"And are you going snowboarding?"

"I think so."

Alone in the house with the news about the twins, I picked up the phone to call Mike and Brooke. *No, Laurie and Bob should have the pleasure of telling them.* One ring and I hung up. I dialed Brenda. *No, if she knows, her four sons will know, and Laurie will find out I told.* One ring and I hung up.

I tried to busy myself, scrubbed and poked holes in two baking potatoes, put them on a sheet pan, slid them into the oven, turned it on. I don't usually start potatoes in a cold oven, but I also don't usually find out my daughter is having twins.

*See? You can make it without telling anyone. Just wait for Henry to get home.*

*It won't hurt to try his cell phone.*

But I got his voicemail and hung up without leaving a message. I didn't trust myself not to blurt out the whole thing.

I took out the salmon fillet I'd bought that morning, spread open the butcher paper. For a split second, I imagined the fish lying on its side, not skinned or filleted, its head still on—one critical, lacquered BB eye staring at me. *You don't understand, Mr. Fish,* I wanted to say. *You don't understand at all. I'm actually the best secret-keeper in the world. Somebody could do slow water torture on me and I would never reveal another person's secret. But my own secret? My own delicious secret? I cannot hold it in.*

I wrapped up the salmon, back in the butcher paper, back in the refrigerator. Too reproachful.

I picked up the phone, dialed Henry again. This time, I left a message, couldn't help it. "Hey. Call me the second you get this. I want to tell you about Laurie and Bob's doctor visit."

And then this thought jumped into my brain: My father was a twin!

But, because he didn't like his twin sister, I didn't think it counted. Aunt Sarah, her husband, and their four children lived only a few blocks away in Rock Hill, that small town, but we hardly ever saw them. My father was not just the dominant twin; he was dominant among all six children. Maybe that wasn't easy for Aunt Sarah. They had a disagreement over money and ethics, ethics being a central issue for my father. In the end, he said that was it for their relationship.

*Let's see now, how does this work? Will Mike and Brooke also have twins?*

The phone! Henry!

"I want you to come straight home," I said, "because I'm dying to tell you about their doctor's visit." I quickly added, "It's all good."

"Just give me a word."

"Twins."

"Yeah, right."

"No, really. They're going to have twins."

"Oh my God! Oh my God! Are you serious? Oh my God! Are you serious? Oh my God!"

Right then, on the phone, Henry standing outside the steam room, probably wrapped in one of those skimpy little Y towels, me in the kitchen, my hands smelling like fish, I told the whole thing—about the uterus and the two tiny circles and the two heartbeats. I didn't leave out a thing.

———

A few days later, Henry was in his office and I was in mine. He had retired the year before. Only a door separated his office (also the guest room) from my office (also the upstairs landing).

He opened his door and walked over to my desk to tell me what he'd just heard on public radio: "A pregnant woman went in for an ultrasound, and the doctor told her she was going to have twins. Weeks passed. She was gaining a huge amount of weight. She kept thinking, 'Something's not right. There's more going on in there . . .'"

I interrupted. "Tell it fast. You're making me nervous."

"They did another ultrasound and found that the two eggs had each divided again and now there were two sets of identical twins. Nothing like that had ever happened in medical history."

———

"Want to know how early a baby becomes identical twins?" Laurie had read up on the subject and was calling to report. "The egg and sperm meet. Then, sometime before the twelfth day of pregnancy, the fertilized egg splits in two. The two halves grow into identical twins. Nobody knows what causes the fertilized egg to split. It's a mystery. Fraternal twins can be genetic or a result of fertility drugs or in vitro fertilization. But identical twins occur totally by chance. Do you know how rare they are? Four per thousand births. .004 percent."

President George W. Bush was quoted in the paper as saying, "I've raised twins and gone to war and of the two, going to war is easier."

Actually, that raises a whole other set of questions.

———

Late afternoon, Henry and I were running errands and, because it was seventy degrees in the middle of winter and we were feeling so good, we decided to go straight from the light bulb aisle in Home Depot to dinner. Never mind the lamb chops I'd thawed that morning. Let's go to Thai Orchid! Every time we just up and decide to eat out at the last minute, my mind shoots back to when Laurie and Mike were little and we would have to plan ahead, call a sitter, feed and bathe the kids before walking out the door. How many years had we looked forward to this freedom?

At dinner I said, "Let's talk about the babies."

Maybe I never really wanted to be free of our children. Maybe all I wanted was to be steeped in them.

"Well," Henry said, "I was thinking the other day that we'll never be able to give one of the twins all our attention. Of course, that might be a good thing."

"You're right," I said. "Just by being a twin, you're conferred a certain specialness. At the same time, you always have to share the spotlight. That's probably the formula for a well-adjusted person. You grow up feeling special, but you know you're not unique."

We folded crisp lettuce leaves around sweet and salty mee krob and shared a bottle of light Thai beer. Diners at tables surrounded us, their quiet buzz. Life slowed. It was one of those rare times when you know what's coming and you're ready.

# 13.

August 18, 2002, the day before Laurie's scheduled C-section. Henry and I packed our largest bags and drove to Durham, planning to stay two months. We had stopped our mail and newspaper, weeded the garden after the usual heat-of-summer neglect, taken care of bills and everything else we could imagine might need our attention. Originally, I'd thought we would stay a month. But a friend of mine, the mother of triplets, called to say she'd heard Laurie was pregnant with twins. "You should stay at least two months," she said, "maybe three."

I can hardly put into words what it felt like, walking into our daughter and son-in-law's house, knowing the purpose of our visit. There was a ... what? A lightness? A density? The renovation had not been finished—that was obvious. Paint cans at the foot of the stairs, a door leaning against a wall, furniture not moved back. But even in the disarray, you could feel a wellspring of possibilities. Reality had veered, and we were all some place we'd never been. How many times in this one life will I find myself someplace I've never been? And how many times will those unfamiliar places end up feeling familiar?

They'd hired a contractor, but he turned out to be a jackleg. Thankfully, he completed enough of the job (converting half the attic into a guest bedroom, bath, and laundry room) that Henry and

I had a comfy place to sleep. But Laurie and Bob had spent the past two days trying to finish up some of what he'd left undone.

Laurie was so swollen she didn't even look like herself. Her feet were pillows. Her hands, which I used to call little baby hands, were hams. Even the delicate features of her face were hidden in puffiness. She was excited. Then calm. Then jumpy. Then awed. Her mood changed minute by minute. As did mine.

Late in the afternoon, that perspiry August day, no rain for weeks, the two women who lived across the street, Margaret and Linde, rang the bell. Margaret had baked a tomato pie, brimming with thick slices of tomatoes from their garden. She was a thin woman, very southern. Linde was sturdy, German. Just as they were about to leave, Linde asked if she could offer a prayer for Laurie and Bob. Before we knew it, the six of us were standing in a circle in that small living room, holding hands, heads bowed. Linde asked God to bestow his blessings on this young couple and help them give birth to two healthy babies. She said a few more sentences and then closed with, "There's joy coming in the morning!"

Henry, Bob, Laurie, and I were all sniffling. It was as though her words caught the light circulating in the dust the contractor had left behind. Normally, I would scoff at the idea of holding hands with strangers and praying in anybody's living room. But Linde's prayer merged with my own.

That night it was hard for Laurie and me to part. She showed me the clothes the babies (my granddaughters!) would wear home from the hospital. (Around the twentieth week of pregnancy, Laurie and Bob had been told they were having girls.) Laurie placed the outfits, side by side, on her white, tufted bedspread, smoothing the sleeves and pants flat with her fingers. For a second, I could picture two little girls—one wearing the red-and-orange-striped outfit and the other, the medium blue with funny bug buttons down the front.

Bob was elsewhere in the house, hanging doors, moving furniture back, touching up paint in the stairwell, which got dinged by the carpet guy. Henry was helping him. No time to install the banister on the stairway. (How many times would I carry two babies up and down the stairs, no banister to hold, brushing my shoulder against the wall to stay steady?) There were many things that would just have to be done later. Much later.

Henry and I, late that night, headed up those banisterless stairs.

———

Laurie and Bob had told us to sleep the next morning and take our time getting to the hospital, that they wouldn't actually do the caesarian till late morning. No need to wake up when they had to, at 4:30 a.m.

But the minute I heard stirrings downstairs, I hopped out of bed, zipped my robe, half skipped down the stairs. I didn't want to miss a minute of the day. Henry was right behind me.

Laurie and Bob were actually on their way out the front door. We hugged them for as long as the clock would allow.

For months, the obstetrician had referred to the twins as Baby A and Baby B, so I'd taken to calling them Alice and Betty. As Laurie and Bob walked down the porch steps to their car—Bob holding a duffel bag in one hand, Laurie's arm in the other—Henry and I stood in the doorway and waved.

"Alice and Betty," I called out, "we'll see you soon!"

We watched till they pulled up to the corner, stopped at the stop sign, turned left onto Roxboro Road. When we could no longer see their taillights, we went back inside and started pulling out cereal boxes—Cheerios for me, GrapeNuts for Henry. But before I reached for a bowl, I hurried upstairs to turn on the shower. Then I turned off the shower and rushed back downstairs to ask Henry to start the coffee. But he had already started the coffee. He was now straightening up the living room, picking up shoes and last night's water glasses. We pinged from one thing to another. Finally, we decided to skip breakfast, just have coffee, forget taking showers, get to the hospital as fast as we could.

Archie, the cat, appeared very nervous. He kept policing the edge of whatever room I was in, and sniffing. Once, when I walked by him, he took a swipe at me, his paw lightning quick. Would he continue to hit me when nobody was around to see? I am not a cat person. It occurred to me to open the front door and let him wander off.

In the middle of our disorder, the phone rang. Henry, in the kitchen, hurried over to answer, but the phone on the counter didn't work. He then ran down the hall to Laurie's office and tried that phone.

"Shit! Shit!" I heard him yelling. He then ran into the living room, looking for another phone. "Shit! Why can't our children just have regular phones? Why do they have this big-deal phone system? And where *are* their phones?"

The phone stopped ringing. We had no idea if it was Bob calling from the hospital with important news.

Now Henry was back in the kitchen, standing at the counter, studying the phone.

"Forget the darned phone," I said. "Let's just go!"

Remember, when something catches Henry's attention, there is no moving him forward. And you will never see him rush. He was now patiently, carefully, turning the phone over in his hand, pressing different buttons. He was going to figure out how to use these phones if it meant he spent the whole day in the kitchen. Babies? What babies?

Another ring. Which startled him.

He picked up.

He must have pushed the speakerphone button somewhere along the way, because I could hear our nephew, Adam, who lives in Raleigh, the youngest of Henry's sister Ruth's four sons. Adam could hardly talk he was laughing so hard. That kind of laughing where you're holding your side.

"Y'all are the keystone grandparents!" he said. "I could hear you cussing, Uncle Henry! And I could hear you running from room to room!"

Henry looked at me; I looked at him. I knew what he was thinking: *We are never going to live this down.*

Henry told Adam which hospital; he and his wife, Cooper, would meet us there. Adam and Laurie had grown up together, close cousins. We finished getting ready. I cut wide circles around Archie, trying not to walk anywhere near him. One of his scratches on my ankle had already drawn blood.

Finally, we were off to Durham Regional.

---

Laurie: In a high hospital bed, that smile, straight white teeth, her smile like glitter, the same smile as in the photographs Henry, the photographer of the family, had taken of her over the years—first-day-of-school pictures, ready-to-blow-out-the-candles pictures, ready-for-prom pictures, and now, ready-to-give-birth pictures. Backward and forward we go.

In that hospital room, there were monitors everywhere, sending out their secret signals. Laurie was clearly happy, and calm. I imagined two babies curled just beneath her heart.

Bob, normally quietly understated, a person of good sense and equanimity, was in such a state of alertness, so keyed up, it looked as if the soles of his shoes were springs. He was past ready for the nurse to tell him it was time to step into his sterile scrubs. When he showed us the papery body suit, mask, hat, gloves, and slippers he would wear, he joked about taking off for outer space.

The door opened, and in walked Mike and Brooke. They'd just driven up from Charlotte. They brought a freshness, a warmth, a party feeling to the room. They were wearing khaki shorts, T-shirts, and Birkenstocks. Their presence filled that antiseptic and unfamiliar room with something familiar. Hugs all around and questions about what had gone on so far. Everyone jokey.

And then, it was time. Bob was told to go into the next room to put on the sterile suit. They were ready to wheel Laurie into surgery.

Out in the hall, we found Laurie and Bob's friends, along with Ruth and her son Adam (*How did he get here so fast? We were just on the phone with him.*) and Cooper. Bob's parents would drive down from Connecticut later.

I was as nervous as I'd ever been in my life.

I left everyone to stand near the door, which I knew not to open. I stood there for a while, letting time pass. I joined the others again. Then I left to stand by the door. Then I joined everyone again. Could not chitchat. Back to the door. This time I opened it a little. Enough to slip into the narrow hall, close to the double-swing doors that led to the operating room. The operating room where Laurie and Bob were. I looked around. Nobody saw me. No nurse to tell me to go back. Good. I stood there, glad to be alone, glad to give in to my fears and think of all the things that could be going wrong in that room.

I pictured myself giving birth to Laurie, my thirty-six-hour labor, the back pain that had turned me inside out. She was occiput posterior, sunny-side up; her head was down, but she faced out. So, despite contractions, I could not dilate. At one point, my parents poked their heads into the labor room, and my father, referring to the old family stories about my slow eating, said, "Well, Judy, you're still eating your green peas one at a time!"

And then, that very minute, I heard a baby's cry.

My daughter's baby's cry!

My granddaughter's cry!

And then I heard another cry.

The second baby!

I ran to tell the others. We were probably too loud for a hospital, but that thought didn't occur to me until much later when I compared this scene to that other scene thirty-three years before. Then, my parents, Brenda and Chuck, Ruth, Mother's sister Aunt Emma, and her daughter Belle were in the waiting area. When Henry came out to tell them it was a girl—this was after my sister and Henry's sister had each given birth to four boys—everyone went berserk. My giving birth to a girl was as much a streak of light as Laurie's giving birth to identical twins! As the nurse wheeled me from Delivery to my room, she wagged her finger at me: "You need to tell your family to pipe down."

Layer on layer. It's hard to turn remembering off.

———

Bob brought out the babies. Tiny bundles of blanket.

Somebody asked, "What are their names?"

"We don't know yet," he said, hoisting them higher.

The babies appeared truly identical. Same round eyes, like Bob's. Same tiny nose, like Laurie's. Tiny pale-rose lips. Bob's lips. He managed to pull back both blankets with one gentle hand, slide off their knit hats, and we saw their coppery-red hair. Electric, it was so bright. Exactly the shade Henry's used to be. My tall, handsome redhead.

"Wow!" we all exclaimed, practically in unison.

"That hair!" somebody said.

"It's really something!"

"Holy cow!"

"Shit!"

———

In Laurie's hospital room, Henry held one baby; I held the other. Then we switched. I reached inside the blanket and touched the baby's toes, those little pieces of fruit. Henry and I joked about how thoughtful it was of Laurie and Bob to provide a baby for each of us to hold. Various friends and relatives came into the room, one at a time, and stayed for a few minutes. Henry snapped a picture of each person sitting in the chair in the corner, holding two babies. Same chair, same babies, same pose, different person.

Henry and I left for a while, got lunch, gave Laurie and Bob time to be alone with the babies.

Late afternoon, we were back, and Laurie said she and Bob had a name announcement. By this time, my sister, Brenda, and her husband, Chuck, had arrived, on their way to Richmond to tour public gardens. Brenda was sitting in the corner chair, holding the babies. Laurie said she wanted to announce the names while Aunt Brenda and Uncle Chuck were there.

Baby A would be named Zoe Amelia Smithwick. Baby B would be Lucy Kurtz Smithwick.

Of course, I teared up hearing that one of the babies would have Kurtz, Brenda's and my maiden name, for her middle name. Laurie knew this would send me reeling. I was happy my sister was with us to hear the news.

But, suddenly and oddly, very oddly, as though my vision were flickering and blurring, I imagined all these people in the room.

*Oh my gosh, the room is overflowing with Kurtzes! Kurtzes everywhere!*

My father! Right there! With us! Okay, maybe I couldn't actually see him. But I could feel his presence. And also, my father's older brother, Albert, standing right beside my father. Mother used to say she thought I'd marry a man like Uncle Albert. She was picturing his sweet and gentle nature. I was picturing his loose, quivery chins, the hearing aid that was always ringing out, his belly round as a moon. "Please!" I would say to Mother, both of us laughing. "Anybody but Uncle Albert!"

My father's older sister, Gertrude, was there. In the room. I still have her photo, covered with bubble glass, that she gave me when I was little, which I eventually tacked to my bulletin board in the den on Eden Terrace, her dance pose, one leg raised behind her, the gypsy costume, wide sash, her tambourine.

And Esther, the oldest of the Kurtz children. Esther married Harry, such a dead ringer for Harry Truman that they caused a stir in the early '50s when they boarded the Queen Mary for Europe. "The president is onboard!" everyone shouted.

My father's older brother, Easy—easygoing, hence his name. Right there.

Of course, I felt Grandma Kurtz beside us. Still stout. Still diabetic. Her wedding band would have fit a very large man, but after sizing it down, I can wear it.

Grandpa Kurtz was with us, also. The scholar. The lover of baseball stats.

Even my father's twin sister, Sarah, was with us. Good. She *should* be with us. Let's get her and my father talking. Not too late for them to make up.

All the Kurtzes, all of us, thrilled with Lucy's middle name.

New life continues to arrive in the space where all those other lives stopped. Families go on. Twins then, twins now, lifetimes away from each other. The past floats forward, then whirls back. As if by magnetic force. This is how the world looked then. This is how the world looks now.

# 16.

Laurie's goal was to nurse both babies at the same time, using the U-shaped pillow (marketed as "My Breast Friend") to place them head to head across her breasts. But it was not easy keeping two infants on the same schedule and, because they were small and needed milk so often and refused to take a bottle, she spent much of the day, and night, nursing one baby or the other or both.

During the night, the first four weeks, Henry and I kept the babies in a Pack 'n Play in our room upstairs. When a baby woke, Henry and I took turns changing her, taking her downstairs, waking Laurie, and sitting with her in the nursery while she nursed.

Oh, how that dreamy wash of light from the lamb night-light made the full presence of mother and baby come at me.

I would ask, "Do you want me to read?"

Laurie always answered, "Yes."

I'd read aloud from one of her books about newborns. Our favorite was the nursing booklet she'd been given in the hospital.

"Okay, listen to this," I said. And I'd read a chapter. Then we talked about it; our back-and-forth made it seem as though caring for twin babies would be easy.

After the feeding, I whisked the baby back upstairs. Henry and I often passed each other on the stairs, him bringing a baby down, me taking a baby up. *Careful, lean your shoulder against the wall.* I burped the baby, then rocked her to sleep, the squeaks of the glider on the landing outside our room like music you commit to memory.

The babies were truly identical. One night, I brought a baby down to nurse, Laurie positioned herself in the rocker, I handed her the baby, settled in across the room ready to read, and she said, "Oh, Mom, I just fed this one!"

We couldn't know then that these so-alike baby girls would some-day become themselves. Zoe, a science person. Lucy, an arts person. Both, singers. Lucy's hair, curly. Zoe's, wavy. Both still very red.

Some nights, Henry and I would lie flat on our backs in our bed up-stairs, each holding a fretful baby on our chest. I sang. He sang. One night, neither of us was singing. We were just patting those babies, rolling our hands a little from place to place as if there were some se-cret spot we could touch to help them be done with their crying. He looked over at me and said, "Can you believe how lucky we are?"

We cradled those faces. Kissed their eyelids. Sang "Take Me Out to the Ballgame" or "Let Me Call You Sweetheart."

Sometimes, in the middle of the night, the babies were so fussy Henry and I took them outside to the wooden slatted swing hanging from the beadboard ceiling on the front porch. We let the night pour cool on all of us, and the babies eventually slept, a spongy cheek nuz-zled into my neck, a spongy cheek nuzzled into Henry's. My long-ago dream come true. I wondered what Margaret and Linde thought, if they happened to glance across the street at three in the morning, the four of us swinging.

We bathed the babies in their yellow plastic tubs side by side on the kitchen counter, took them for walks in the double stroller, mak-ing U-turns to avoid streets where the sun might flare up in their eyes. Usually, partway through the walk, they both wanted out of the stroller, so one of us would push the empty stroller, while the other carried two babies the rest of the way home. We were awfully good at tenderness.

When Lucy and Zoe were three weeks old, Bob's parents drove down from Connecticut for a week's visit. Henry grocery shopped, and I cooked a big lasagna dinner for all of us the night they arrived. Then after dinner Henry and I drove back to Charlotte to give Bob's parents a chance to be with their new granddaughters, without us hovering. I knew that Bob's mom would do anything to help, but would she think to bring a tall glass of water, no ice, to Laurie every hour or so? My daughter, nursing two babies, nonstop. And would she make sure Laurie was snacking frequently? My daughter nursing two babies, nonstop. No one takes care of a daughter like her own mother—or, at least, no one could know what it means to take care of this particular daughter.

My week back home, all I could do was cook. It's what grandmothers do. Or, at least, it's my idea of what grandmothers do. You can worry. Or you can cook. Just keep sifting flour, chopping garlic, sautéing boneless chicken breasts. All to go into Laurie's freezer when we get back to Durham. *How is Laurie doing?* Bake date nut bars. *How is Zoe doing?* Pick basil from the garden and make pesto. *How is Lucy doing?* Slide a chicken casserole into the oven.

When I was little, I not only aspired to grandparenthood, I also aspired to be the kind of cook my grandchildren would cook with. I pictured us making biscuits together in my steamy kitchen, the scent of buttermilk, a sift of flour everywhere. Pictured myself the grandmother whose soup and pies they'd remember the rest of their lives. I do cook. But I'm not *that* cook. Not a memorable cook.

———

My friend since sixth grade, Marilee, says she's not that type of cook either.

But here she is, eighty, wise, a Marcus Aurelius fan, a widow before she turned fifty, longtime resident of Alexandria, Virginia, retired executive assistant to a progressive U.S. congressman from South Carolina, yoga instructor, mother of two married children, grandmother of five. This is what she says about aging: "I love it! I love it! I love it! Now that I'm eighty, I don't have to bring anything to the holiday dinner! No more salads! Oh, God, I made so many salads!"

———

My fear before we went to Durham was that Laurie and Bob and Henry and I would get on each other's nerves. Four adults and two newborns in one small bungalow—surely, disaster. The week before the babies were born, I brought up the subject with my Breakfast Group:

"How will we all manage? In such close quarters? With newborns? For such a long time?"

They were ready with advice. I took a notepad from my purse and jotted down their tips:

1. *No eye-rolling or sarcastic remarks.*
2. *Use affectionate gestures.*
3. *There will be a low point—there always is—when things fall apart.*
4. *You're only there to take care of the babies, do the laundry, grocery shop, and cook. You should never offer advice on any subject.*
5. *No matter what's going on, you don't get a vote.*

The low point, when things fell apart:

One morning, only a couple of weeks into our stay, I was changing Lucy's diaper in the nursery, and I saw a red blotch on her bottom.

"Laurie," I called out, "come look at this."

"Yeah, I saw it," she said, strolling into the nursery, then strolling out again, not in a hurry either way. "Probably diaper rash."

"No," I said, raising my voice so that she could hear me, no matter where in the house she was headed. I heard the clink of hangers; she was in her bedroom. "It's *definitely* not diaper rash. I've seen a *lot* of diaper rash, and this is definitely *not* diaper rash." I'd just gotten Lucy up from her morning nap and she was still sleepy, so she was lying quietly on the cushioned chest of drawers. Every now and then, a soft little kick.

I knew I was being overbearing and violating the Breakfast Group's Rule #4 and Rule #5. But I was alarmed by that red whatever-it-was.

"I think a doctor ought to take a look at this," I said, coating Lucy's bottom with Desitin, knowing cream would do no good.

"Well, why don't we just wait a day or two and see if it disappears?" Laurie was now in her office. She was probably checking her email.

"It could get worse." I was now yelling. Lucy was looking up at me, her little face lit by the sun slanting through the blinds.

"If we wait a day?"

"I've seen things get worse in an hour."

"Mom!"

"Laurie! Maybe you should at least call."

I heard her pick up the phone on her desk, punch in the numbers.

Now, she was asking to speak to a nurse, and then I heard her describing the blotch. She wasn't describing it as fully as I thought she should.

"Tell how it wasn't there and then, all of a sudden, it was. Tell them it's definitely *not* diaper rash." *Why can't I just press my lips together and be quiet?*

"Uh-*huh*," I heard her say, apparently agreeing with what the nurse was saying.

Laurie hung up but did not come back into the nursery. Henry had gotten Zoe up earlier and had her in the living room. I could hear him reading to her. By this time, I had Lucy in a fresh onesie, white with a yellow duck on the front, and I was wrapping her in a blanket, then holding her high on my shoulder, on my way into the living room.

Now I heard Laurie in her bedroom. She was opening drawers, not exactly slamming them shut, but a degree more firmly than just closing them. She was muttering, "The nurse says to watch it and call back in a few days if it's not gone."

It did not go away in a few days. It got worse.

The next week, Laurie and Bob took the girls for their one-month check-up. The doctor said it was a hemangioma, a collection of blood vessels that grows at first, then stays the same, then disappears. Lucy now had a second hemangioma on the tip of her nose, and Zoe had one just inside her left nostril. "They'll be gone," the pediatrician said, "by the time the girls are two or three." Nothing to worry about, she said. Nothing at all to worry about.

———

4. *You're only there to take care of the babies, do the laundry, grocery shop, and cook. You should never offer advice on any subject.*
5. *No matter what's going on, you don't get a vote.*

———

At the end of two months, Laurie and Bob floated the idea of our staying another month. They said they did not want to take advantage of us and would understand if we were ready to go home. But would we consider holding off leaving?

I was perfectly willing to stay one more month.

Henry wasn't so sure.

"Don't you think it's time for us to get back to our own lives?" he said to me that night in bed. A rhetorical question.

"Laurie would never leave me in this fix," I said. "How can I leave her?"

For several weeks, we'd been returning to Charlotte on Friday to give them a chance to go it alone for the weekend. I convinced Henry to stay one more month, but agreed we could start leaving Durham even earlier on Friday—sometimes Thursday—and we could return later on Sunday—sometimes Monday.

———

One Sunday night when we returned, Bob ushered us into the nursery, which exuded the perfume of babies sleeping. Since their birth, Lucy and Zoe had let us know they would only fall asleep if they were in the same crib, burrowing into each other. I suppose they'd been so fused in the womb, they wanted to stay fused out here. But tonight, there they were, each in her own crib, eyelids closed, thin as petals. Bob was pointing and grinning, that great smile of his, the two babies sleeping, proof that all four of them were adjusting to their new lives.

Truth is, we were glad Laurie and Bob were making it on their own. We didn't mind getting back to our house. We were ready to wake up in our own bed to the morning light sifting through our bamboo shades. We were ready for the phone to ring and have it be *our* friends. We were ready to pick up shampoo at our drugstore, walk to Ben and Jerry's after dinner, mulch the azaleas. I was ready to write again. Henry was ready for racquetball at the Y. It was time. The babies had been weaned off us; Laurie and Bob had been weaned off us.

All that was left: to wean us off them.

# *17.*

I wondered if I could possibly form the same kind of bond with future grandchildren that I had with Lucy and Zoe. After all, I'd lived with the twins the first three months of their lives, given them their first baths, been there when they woke in the middle of the night, was the face they saw after naps, fed them their first solid food.

Also, friends who already had grandchildren from both daughters and daughters-in-law warned me that the involvement is different when it's your son's baby. Your daughter-in-law's mother is naturally the primary grandparent. A daughter usually wants her own mother, after all.

But.

The next baby would be Mike's.

Mike, who is more like me than anyone alive, whose feelings I often believe I can feel, they're so similar to my own. We can look at each other and immediately see the motive behind each other's motive. He's always saying, "Mom, I know you understand what I mean." I say the same to him. Our temperaments match—balanced, levelheaded—and we each get unduly vexed when things don't seem fair. We set goals and usually meet those goals because we never set unreachable goals. And we always have a backup. Our instincts, how we just *know* certain things in certain situations with certain people. We've always had such a powerful and secure bond. How could I not have the same with his baby?

————

Mike and Brooke started dating when they were students at the University of Richmond. After graduating, they moved in together in Winston-Salem, where Brooke earned a master's in psychology at Wake Forest University and Mike began his career as a financial advisor. A couple of years later, they surprised us by moving to Charlotte. Brooke is intuitive, a good listener (she zeroes in on you, eyeball to eyeball), and she gives great advice. She's also lighthearted and lively, will always be the one to bake an elaborate birthday cake, organize a board game after family dinner, shoot fireworks on the beach. She has such smooth olive skin that when she invited me to go wedding shopping with her and her mom, I told her to be sure to choose a gown that showed plenty of skin.

Mike is a person who does not fill the air with talk, but when he says something, you can bet it will be wise or witty, depending on what's called for. About the witty part, he's probably the funniest person I know. And, he is gentle and kind. *And*—this is not just because I'm his mother and prejudiced—he's good-looking.

Of course, when Mike and Brooke's Tess was born, I immediately felt as tied to her as I felt to Lucy and Zoe. It was instant. My worry about a remove, a loose connection, was forgotten the second I saw her. When I held her, it felt like heaven in my hands. How naive I'd been, how silly, how utterly unaware of the way each child—even if I should be lucky enough to live to see my grandchildren grow up and give birth to their own children—curls one finger around your heart and will not let go.

All those times with Tess as she was growing up—the two of us drawing together, her artistic eye, her drawings vivid with color, her attention to detail. How she loved being busy—soccer, horseback riding, rock climbing. Her early years, she wanted to play hide-and-seek every time she came over. The inventive hiding places she found, under the skirted table next to our bed—she was small enough then and clever enough to know I'd never find her folded around the table legs. I believe she was six when she fell in love with baking. For Hanukkah one year, I gave her a cupcake cookbook. We spent an entire Saturday turning out penguin cupcakes, their proud black-and-white tuxedos, pointy yellow beaks, orange feet, beady eyes. Dozens of tasty penguins squatting on every surface in my kitchen.

———

It all began with a breathless phone call on February 17, 2005, from Mike, letting us know Brooke had gone into labor.

Henry and I rushed to the same hospital where I'd given birth to both Mike and Laurie. We sat in the luxurious, light-filled waiting room—why do hospitals spend so much money on waiting rooms?—with Brooke's parents (in from Asheville) and Laurie (in from Durham), and we waited, and we waited, each of us calling various relatives and friends on our cell phones, saying *No, not yet, still waiting.*

And then, even when Mike came out, there was more waiting—because he just stood there, star-eyed, not able to say a word. We all jumped up, surrounded him, five of us in a tight circle around him. I believe his lips might have been moving, but no sound escaped. In the photos Laurie took, we're all leaning in to Mike, all standing at such a slant it looks as if we could pull the words, one at a time, from his throat.

Finally, he spoke, smiling that smile of his, which you cannot help but meet with a smile; it's that infectious: "It's a girl! And we named her Tess! And she's fine! And Brooke's fine!"

We went crazy with joy. We hugged him, all of us at once. Then he pointed two index fingers (like someone directing an airplane to the gate) in the direction of the delivery room and again seemed unable to speak. He just kept pointing, pointing. Finally, haltingly, as though he wasn't sure where he should go because he wasn't sure where he was—that tall, lean, normally self-assured son of ours—he said, "I should probably get back." He sort of choked on the word *back*. Then he was gone.

The next thing was when we all crowded into the room where two nurses were still tending to Brooke and the baby—very busy nurses, and we were happily oblivious to the fact that we might be getting in their way—and Mike held Tess and we exclaimed about her lovely, round head and her awning of eyelashes and ripe-peach lips (like Mike's), and we took turns holding her and talking baby-talk, the glassy music of that language, and then Brooke—looking as relaxed as though she had not just given birth, her smile, the one where she wrinkles her nose, her eyes rimmed in lashes she'd already passed down to her daughter—was telling us how the night before (eight days after her due date), she had made the special eggplant parmesan recipe famous for bringing on the birth of a late baby and amazingly, she'd gone into labor not long afterward. Somebody was snapping pictures—don't remember who, just remember not having to consciously smile for them because I was already smiling—and Brooke took the baby, so close to her ribs, and we were even crazier with joy, that thick rush of something you can hardly think of a name for.

———

That thick rush again, three years later, January 19, 2008, when Brooke was in labor once more, ready to give birth. We all rushed to the same hospital where Tess had been born. Once again, we waited. Once again, we were crazy with joy when the baby arrived. And his name! Benjamin! Named for his great-grandfather! My father! But I didn't have time to imagine all the Kurtzes swarming into that hospital, though they *would* have come, how thrilled they would be, once again. But this time, excitement was quickly replaced by worry.

Baby Benjamin was born with Group B strep (GBS), a bacterial infection a baby can catch from the mother during childbirth. GBS infection usually does not cause any problems in healthy women, but it can cause serious illness in newborns. About one in four pregnant women have GBS in their birth canal.

Benjamin was immediately whisked to the neonatal intensive care unit, where he would be closely monitored.

I can still see the handwashing station at the entrance of the NICU, those clear and ominous instructions on just how long you should scrub, the bulletin board over the sink pinned with snapshots of babies who'd started life there and were now thriving.

I can see in my mind Benjamin's little bassinette with its opening just big enough to reach through to change his diaper or pat his dimpled hand, tubes and wires everywhere.

I spent hours in the NICU, in a rocker, holding Benjamin in my arms or just sitting close to the bassinette, touching his hand. One morning, Mike showed me how to change his diaper. "Like this, Mom," he said, as he reached through the little opening and whisked off the old diaper and fastened the crisp new diaper. As though it was the most natural thing in the world, in this very unnatural world where we found ourselves. I was struck, trancelike, by the ease with which he did this very delicate thing so smoothly, here, in this strained place, some kind of harmony at work. The two of them—my son and his son.

Then it was time for me to change the diaper. Timidly, with the tips of my fingers, I shifted the tubes and IV lines out of the way. My hands were shaking. I think I even felt a little dizzy from the responsibility. But I got it done. And I believe I soon became used to it. Then again, maybe I never got used to it. Maybe I changed only one diaper. Tiny baby, need to be careful, serious consequences if you make a mistake, so precarious. Mostly, I sat in the rocker and held him close or sat beside the bassinette, imagining holding him close, either way singing softly, "Take Me Out to the Ballgame" or "Let Me Call You Sweetheart."

Even in that setting, even amidst the unease, even half hidden by tubes and wires, the beauty of his little face beamed out, his complexion smooth and olive like his mother's, his eyes bright and clear, thick lashes like his older sister's.

I asked the nurses and doctors a million questions, so many that one doctor said to me, with genuine interest and not a trace of sarcasm, "Are you in health care?" That was a truly hilarious question, because everyone who knows me knows I am very interested in all things medical and, if truth be told, I'm rather arrogant about my medical instincts.

Once, years before, in the ER, late, late at night, after I'd explained to a physician Henry's symptoms and what I thought the tests they'd run would show and what I thought should be the priorities in treating him, the doctor studied my face—a big, friendly smile on *his* face—and said, "You have the same degree as my wife."

Of course, I asked, "What degree is that?"

"AAD," he said. He waited a few seconds before going further. He was just as skilled at the comedic pause as he was at doctoring. "Almost A Doctor."

I did not need to call on my AAD degree in the NICU. Not for a minute. Those doctors and nurses were competent, attentive, caring—just superb. The morning Benjamin was discharged, I told them that if and when I end up in the hospital, I hope I get a bed in the NICU.

Our fourth grandchild. Our first grandson. Benjamin. At thirteen, he will be so in love with sports stats, he'll write an ongoing blog to advise subscribers which players to pick in Fantasy Football. At fifteen, he'll broadcast school sporting events. His knowledge of sports will be that solid. That clear, strong voice telling facts, describing plays, cracking jokes.

Sports stats.

From his great-great-grandfather to his great-grandfather to his grandfather to his father to him.

How grandchildren make sense of our mortality, one generation giving way to the next, and the next. It goes on. We keep seeing ourselves. That complex configuration of chromosomes tracking across ages.

# 18.

t's 2021. My friend Kathryne calls, driving home to Bethune, a small town in South Carolina where her mother's family has lived for generations. She lives in the house her mother grew up in and where her parents were married. She sleeps in the room where her mother died, six weeks after Kathryne's fourth birthday. My friend since nursery school, Kathryne is eighty and wholeheartedly upbeat, a retired teacher, widow for eight years (her husband was my childhood friend, also), no children, a former navy wife, which meant she and Freddy lived all over the world. (And remember, she was May Queen and Miss Hi Miss.) She has just spent Christmas Day in Rock Hill with her sister's family.

"Okay! Let's talk about aging!" she says, her voice full of bounce. I had emailed her, asking for her thoughts, and she's ready to deliver.

"After Freddy died, I didn't want to do anything. You don't want to leave where you feel safe. Your little nest. But then, I was ready to do things. My Birthday Club—it's my group of teacher friends from San Diego, like your Breakfast Group, Judy—had made plans to travel to Hawaii. But everything got cancelled because of Covid."

I tell her about Laurie J.'s comments, about wishing she still wanted to do things.

"I'm the exact opposite! I'm alive! Half the people I know are dead! I still want to do things! I was ready to go, then the Covid Delta variant. I was ready to go, then Omicron. It's turning eighty during a pandemic that has changed *my* life. I feel cheated!"

"Would you still ski?" I ask.

"Yes, I would ski! I still have my skis! I just need to find somebody who'll ski *with* me!"

"Well," I say, "that would not be me."

———

Let's talk about the years Covid sent us back into our homes and made us stay there. For a person who's forty-something, one or two years means nothing. There's always the next year. Nobody is going anywhere. I don't mean that a forty-year-old isn't missing out on a whole lot of living. It's just that the difference between forty-one and forty-two is not significant. The years, around that age, are just years. Not heavy markers.

To an eighty-year-old, which is me, and an eighty-two-year-old, Henry, a year or two is quite a significant measure of time. Mainly because there will not always be a next year.

I think back to who I was before the pandemic. I had just finished a pretty extensive tour for my book *Together: A Memoir of a Marriage and a Medical Mishap*, published in 2019. All that dashing about. Then, in late January 2020, it came out in paperback, which meant another book tour. I'd bought two new sweaters and a scarf; the pants I already owned would be fine.

Everything was set.

Then cancelled.

When I think about book tours, I marvel at my stamina—driving all over the South, finding my way to libraries in small mountain towns where the GPS on my phone doesn't work, spending the night in hotels close enough to I-85 to hear trucks, remembering the name of the event planner who greets me at the next bookstore, keeping track, keeping up, keeping going.

Yes, I can do it again. I'll do it for every book I write. But. How easily I wear myself down these days of the pandemic. Something about it makes me very tired.

*Need to grocery shop. That's about all I can do today.*

*Oh dear. Friday will be very busy. Ten o'clock Zoom call with friends.*

*A virtual funeral tomorrow. Cancel everything else.*

Just one thing on my calendar, and I'm ready to collapse on the sofa, watch Netflix, eat caramel popcorn.

Virtual funerals. We act as though this is a perfectly normal thing. Kinship clumsily memorialized on a screen.

My friend, Thea, and I met the first day of our freshman year at the University of Georgia. We lived down the hall from each other in South Myers dorm. Then we roomed together our sophomore year with two other friends—two sets of saggy bunk beds upstairs in our creaky old sorority house. Thea had a smoker's voice, a big laugh, dated only good-looking boys, and had the neatest sock drawer I'd ever seen. She's the one who talked me into moving to New York City. For years, she and I laughed about her backing out to get married. She always joked, "I should have gone to New York!" She and her husband, Howie, were married fifty-five years. They died five days apart, both from Covid. His virtual funeral was at two o'clock Thursday afternoon; she died Friday morning.

Here we are, pandemic or no pandemic, years flying by, Henry and I, along with the friends of ours who are left. We're just about done with our feverish business on this earth, stalled at the intersection of now and next. The story of each year written on a Kleenex.

# 19.

Phone call with Marilyn, eighty—my first friend after I married Henry and settled in Charlotte (she now lives in Boulder), former Planned Parenthood counselor. She was married to the rabbi at Charlotte's conservative synagogue but left him for Stan, to whom she's been married thirty-nine years. Marilyn and Stan's affair caused a major scandal in the 1970s. They have six daughters and thirteen grandchildren between them. My spirited friend's thoughts:

"At some level, aging and dying are front and center in my mind. So many people in my circle of friends... and my circle is large because I've lived so many places... of course, the more people you know, the more joy you experience and, also, the more pain... but so many people in my circle of friends have either died or are struggling with serious illnesses. And then I wonder... am I going to be like them tomorrow?"

———

I call Lew, seventy-seven, Dannye's husband, whose wry wit and knowledge of random facts delight his friends, retired newspaper journalist, advocate for the wrongfully prosecuted defendants in the Little Rascals Day Care case of the early '90s. I go through my usual request—your thoughts on aging, just your off-the-cuff thoughts, whatever you come up with will be perfect—and he says (typical of a writer who needs to get things down on paper to see what he thinks), "Let me mull this over. Can I just email you some thoughts?" Even though I've been strict with everyone else, I say okay.

Lew's email:

I'm always startled to hear myself recalling something that happened FIFTY years ago. (ME? Really?)

I remember my father saying, "Old men always think the world is going to hell."

The more I look back, the more I realize that I've gotten to this point almost entirely by crazy chance—one unmarked fork in the road after another after another . . .

I'm really OK with mortality. It's morbidity that chills me . . .

As sad as I've felt to lose friends—too many, too young! —there's something almost comforting in being reminded that this is how this world works . . . and that it'll have its way with me as well . . .

If you know the secret to eternal life, don't tell me . . .

I can't imagine not being anchored by my marriage. But there's no denying that one of us will come to sleep alone in our double bed . . . (And our men's lunch group, absent replenishing, won't always need a double table . . . or even a four top) . . .

Here's what I notice about old people's reactions to losing peripheral family members or friends: we're less affected by these deaths than we would have been when we were younger. I'm not talking about a husband dying, or a wife, or child. I'm talking about the death of a cousin, a friend, neighbor, colleague. Someone you cared about but didn't consider central in your life.

This morning a friend texted me to say that Sally died. Now I didn't know Sally very well, but I used to run into her at the county market. We both shopped there because they have the best, most acidic summer tomatoes in town. We'd stand at the counter—so many choices, Heirloom, Early Girl, Big Boy—and we'd fill our little brown paper bags and chat. She was a literary agent—a literary agent in Charlotte, North Carolina! I always admired how innovative she was to be in *that* business in *this* locale. We talked books. She asked about my writing. I asked about her business. I don't know her family, so I hesitate writing a note expressing condolences. Sally is the one I would write to. But Sally is the one who died. I'm sad that I will no longer visit with her at the tomato counter. Her death feels—what? Cumulative? There are more and more of these. One after the other.

Losing *anyone* when we were younger—in our forties, fifties, or sixties—was more than just a sad lapse. It was a cold slap.

When I was forty-six, my good friend took her own life. Betty Jo had come by my house for a quick visit the night before. Sitting at my kitchen table, talking about her deep distress, she said, "I just don't think I can keep going." I still remember, and regret, my reply: "You'll keep going, Betty Jo. You're a strong person." I don't remember what she said next. She just sat there, her big, dark eyes filled with sadness. The next day, two of our friends and Betty Jo and I were supposed to meet at Tio Montero for lunch. Instead, Betty Jo drove to an abandoned drive-in theater on the other side of town and put a bullet in her head. On and on, my friends and I recited the few details we knew—the lottery tickets she'd purchased and left on the front seat of her car, the violets she'd picked and arranged in small vases around her living room. When we weren't cross-examining every detail, we were crying big gulping sobs. We were half buried ourselves, in our sorrow. Everything that could possibly change had changed.

When someone dies now? It's a hard moment, yes. And we hurt. But we go on stirring the soup on the stove, making sure the barley doesn't stick to the bottom of the pot. We go on smearing our lips with gloss. We hold a hand mirror, turn from the larger bathroom mirror, so that we can see to comb the back of our hair. We know it's a dead giveaway of old age, not checking to see how our hair looks when we walk away. We all know the older woman, beautifully turned out, well dressed, makeup just right, who leaves and we see the hair at her crown, mashed flat from sleep or sticking up like an old broom, revealing her pink scalp and her forgetfulness.

Why don't these deaths nest in our core the way they did when we were younger? Why don't they goose our hearts the way they used to?

The obvious explanation is that our peers who died when we were younger were younger themselves. Of course, it's more tragic to lose a young person than an old person. When an old person dies, we say, "Well, he lived a good, long life." But I think there's more to it than how old a person happens to be when they die.

Maybe religion plays a part, although I'm not sure how. People who believe in an afterlife are comforted by the expectation that they'll meet the people they love again. And the older we are when we lose the people we love, the closer we are to the time we'll reunite with them (in heaven?). Death probably feels like less of an interruption to the relationship if we're planning to see the person again soon. I'm not sure what I believe. Where the dead go or don't go. I do believe we live on through our children and grandchildren. But what does that mean? It really makes no sense at all. I understand why people turn to religion. It helps you see an intentional design to your life, created by someone or something out there or up there. And the religious rituals and traditions—even hymns, an integral part of rituals and traditions—are soothing. Mainly, religion helps you cope with your fear of death. You don't worry about dying if you know you're on your way to heaven. My quibble with religion is how it divides us, separates us into teams that can turn territorial. Even adversarial. Regardless, religion or no religion, the question lingers: How do we even begin to fathom that every one of us will vanish into nothingness?

Maybe it's just that we're now accustomed to counting on our fingers the number of bodies that have dropped. Repetition can wear away anything. Even the pang of endings. It's easy to let our guard down when we've been here before. Not that we become casual about death. We still miss people. And their deaths will always remind us of our own death—no denying that. But funerals are no longer a novelty. Maybe we're so used to death that we've grown tired of it.

My friend Kathryne goes to more funerals than anyone. She knows just about everyone in her town, Bethune, so naturally, she attends all their funerals. Jokingly, I tell her I want her to be in charge of my funeral because she, more than anybody, would know how to put on a good one.

If Kathryne dies before me, it will be a totally different kind of experience from anything I've described here, because it will be mixed with excitement and curiosity. When we were eleven, we made a pact that when one of us dies, the other will try to communicate across the void. We even set a day and time for our reunion. The first Wednesday following the death, at five o'clock. We picked Wednesday because I had tap on Monday and ballet on Thursday, and piano was sometimes on Tuesday, sometimes Friday. Wednesdays were free. We picked five o'clock because we were both home by late afternoon, no matter what after-school lessons we had.

I worry a little telling you this. Don't try to interfere with our communication. Just forget you know this. It's an agreement between two people who've been friends since we were four years old. We don't want a lot of strangers horning in. We're truly hoping that our arranged date—whether it's far off or close at hand—will bring the two of us back together.

## 20.

John (Laurie J.'s husband) is a retired pediatrician and also retired from being the first medical director of Teen Health Connection, which serves adolescents who're not receiving routine health care. He would be your ideal pediatrician, sweet-tempered and kind-hearted. Twenty-five years ago, he had a liver transplant, which he believes colors his feelings about aging.

"Here I am, an eighty-year-old guy with someone else's liver. I'm aware that I'm lucky to be alive. Since 1997, I've been living on borrowed time.

"This is probably universal, but I look at my body and I can see wrinkles and moles and things growing on me. And...I used to be so sure-footed. I climbed ladders, hauled rocks, cleared out walking trails in the woods at our family farm. Now I look at myself from the macro viewpoint and I think, *Who the hell is that?* I'm walking down the stairs like an old man. I hold on to the railing, go so slow. It's shocking."

And here's the U-turn:

"In spite of all this, it's a natural process. And that's reassuring. I'm in the flow. We're born, we grow, we develop, we age, we die. That's just what we humans do."

Two years later, John would die of liver failure. Over and over, I'll think of his words, "That's just what we humans do."

———

Paul, a sixty-six-year-old retired ER doctor, now novelist and memoirist, read this memoir to give me feedback. He made his own comment on aging. In the margin beside John's words, he wrote: "None of the guys lamented having to shave their ears?"

———

I was in a hurry a few weeks ago, on my way from my office (our little TV room) to the kitchen, where I'd left my cell phone, which was ringing, ringing, ringing. Just as I got to the kitchen, my foot hit a slippery spot and shot out from under me—a clean, feathered *swoosh!*—and I fell backward, hard, on the floor. My head banged against the wooden door of the cabinet holding the trash and recycling bins.

Suddenly, a high-speed realization: Was I now in a new life? A moment I'd forever think of as between before it happened and after it happened? Was I on my way to the hospital? *Now I've done it! Broken my hip!* How would I take care of Henry if I needed taking care of? This was not good.

But it didn't feel like I'd broken my hip. More likely, I broke my head. It was pounding. *Boing, boing, boing.* A crazy quilt of pain. Kaleidoscopic. Something jammed. How many different ways were there to describe this? As though I was rehearsing what I'd tell Henry and our children. I'm a word person, so I sure as heck needed to figure out how to express what it felt like.

No blood anywhere—that's good. I reached up—also good; I could move my arm. I lightly traced a loop around the place on my head where it hurt. I couldn't bear down. That would have *killed.*

But just barely—barely—I drew circles around and around with one careful finger. I was okay. Maybe I was not okay.

I called out, "Henry!"

"What happened?" he called back from the bedroom or his closet or the bathroom, had to be one of those because he was as far away as he could be in this small, compact condo of ours.

"Are you coming? I need you. I fell."

"I'm coming." Which meant he'd get there, not quickly, but, for sure, as soon as he could. I heard the cane. The thumping. His uneven walk. Heavy foot, not-so-heavy foot, heavy foot, not-so-heavy foot. It sounded as though he was casually strolling, ambling, moseying. Remember, you will never see Henry actually hurry. That's been true of him forever. More so now with his mobility problems.

I didn't move. I just lay there, as though I knew you should not leave the scene of an accident, that it's important for someone—a policeman, a fireman, a husband—to see exactly where things landed.

Maybe what I was thinking is that, after an accident, you shouldn't move too quickly because you could make something worse. A broken arm or leg.

Henry appeared beside me, took both my hands, and gently pulled me up. I stood—upright! My hip was fine, my legs were fine, my back was fine. "I'm okay," I said. But my head still throbbed.

He turned me toward him, started asking me concussion questions. Yes, I did have a headache. But I was not confused, and my speech was not slurred. And I was not dizzy. I felt teary, yes, but that wasn't unusual for me. I'm an easy crier. He left me and went to get a flashlight from the laundry room. I steadied myself with one hand on the kitchen island. When he returned, he shone the light in one eye, moved it away, other eye, then away.

"Pupils are dilating and constricting fine, both the same," he said. Still Mr. Eye Doctor. Although his stroke two years before had affected his balance and coordination, his short- and long-term memory, he could dip right into his knowledge of anything having to do with vision. "That's good," he said.

Later, a few hours after my fall, I felt two big knots on my head. Did I hit the cabinet twice? Did my head bounce, hit, then hit again? A surprise: The entire area around my left elbow was blackened and swollen. Now I could hardly move my arm. But I knew it wasn't broken. It would've hurt much worse. Three fingers on my right hand were also blackened and swollen.

It was getting late. A glance out the French doors and I saw a sky turning blacker by the minute—like my arm and fingers. I asked Henry what we should do about dinner. He said, "Let's just get takeout. You sure don't need to cook."

"But I don't feel like driving anywhere to get it," I said.

He had forgotten he was no longer driving. Or maybe, in the tumult of my fall, he was hoping I'd forgotten he was no longer driving. Since his stroke, I've taken over the driving, a decision he did not participate in and was not happy about. After all, this is the guy whose summer job during grad school in Chicago was driving a city bus, who loved to drive and did not want to give it up. Of course, he would never suggest that I get in a car and drive somewhere after a fall. I was not even walking very solidly.

"How about if you fix eggs and toast?" I said, wanting to avoid the driving topic altogether. "Breakfast for dinner always feels like comfort food."

I thought I would just get him started, make it easy for him. Then he could take over, and I'd go lie down.

I opened the corner cabinet, found the right-size pan, opened the utensil drawer, took out a spatula, the plastic one I use for non-stick pans. From the refrigerator, eggs and butter. Then the freezer and two slices of sourdough bread. I found the little green bowl in the same corner cabinet and a whisk in the same utensil drawer. I dropped a wedge of butter into the fry pan and turned the flame to low. Cracked the eggs into the bowl, whisked till they paled.

Henry was standing beside me, watching, like someone who'd step in and take over any minute. He *wanted* to take over, but I think he was unsure when. Maybe he was thinking I was in such a whirl, he didn't know how to break in. If it's possible to do nothing but look as though you're willing to do anything, that would have been him right then.

"Why don't you set the table?" I said. "Forks and knives and napkins. Strawberry preserves for you, cherry for me. Also, water. Not so much ice for me."

Young Henry would have just taken over. Middle-aged Henry would have taken over. No matter how frenetically and self-righteously and martyrdly I moved around that kitchen. But this is our story now. And we're learning how to make do.

But, oh, we've got the rest of our lives to get through. That's the thought that keeps me up at night. Recently, I read about a great mantra to say to myself when the world strikes four and I'm tossing and turning and the sheet is wrapped around one leg and I'm trying to straighten my nightgown and flip my pillow to the cool underside. But mainly, when I'm just trying to stop obsessing over how, if something happens to me, Henry will have to take care of me when he can barely take care of himself, and if something happens to him, I'll have to take care of him when I can barely take care of myself. My new mantra: "I've already worried about that."

Things will only get worse. Accidents will happen. We'll get sick.

We'll find ourselves in peril. Henry used to be so big and able-bodied and brave. That barrel chest. Thick neck. Hairy arms. I was small, not able-bodied, not brave. I used to joke that I did the same thing Patty Hearst did—married my bodyguard.

Our first year of marriage, we kept a portable TV on a small table in our bedroom. The V-shaped antennae reached up like two arms. On the wall over the TV hung a dark painting of a man's head. Often, in the middle of the night, I saw, with my blurry eyes, the TV, the antennae, and the painting and believed it was a man, in our apartment, arms raised, ready to pounce, ready to rape. Over and over, I told Henry that if I suddenly dug my fingernails into his shoulder at three in the morning, he should not react. "Don't jump or indicate in any way that I've signaled you. Just know I'm letting you know there's an intruder in our bedroom and you need to get rid of him."

In his forties, Henry won the city racquetball championship. He came in third in the state, losing in the semifinals to a guy named Gar Wilde. (Who could ever beat anyone named Gar Wilde?)

But Henry has shrunk four inches in height and lost muscle mass. He is no longer the man who would lunge at an intruder and overpower him. No longer a champ on the racquetball court. No longer even *on* the racquetball court. No longer the man I thought would take care of me forever. *Wait. I've already worried about that.*

I'm not the person he married either. I'm even more of a worrier than I was before, can't shake off my fears. I check the rearview and side mirrors a thousand times before changing lanes. I'm acutely aware of blind spots, on and off the road. Honestly, I can just *see* the upcoming crash. I have it in me to scare myself to death. And I nag. And I'm forgetful. But then, I've always been forgetful. Benjamin loves the story I tell about when he was two and he and Tess were spending the weekend with us. My instructions from Brooke: Change Benjamin into pajamas for his afternoon nap. But I decided to make it easy for myself, and I changed only his diaper. I left on his corduroy pants and long-sleeved T-shirt, lifted him into the crib in our guest room, covered him with his blanket, tucked the stuffed whatever-he-was-sleeping-with-at-the-time beneath his shoulder, into his neck, told him a story, have a good nap, see you soon, turned out the light, night-light beaming from the corner, closed the door, headed downstairs. I got as far as the kitchen when I heard him calling: "Dayday! Dayday!" (His version of Gaygay, the name Lucy and Zoe had given me when they couldn't say Grandmommy.) I rushed upstairs to see what was wrong. He was standing in the crib, holding his blanket and his stuffed whatever. "You fordot my padamas! Dayday, you fordet evwyting."

Add to all that, I now fall.

There are more years to get through. How many, we don't know. My guess is, Henry and I will probably manage okay. Not the okay I envisioned back when we stood under the orchid- and ivy-covered chuppah at our wedding, in front of the windows in my parents' living room, our twenty-eight smiling guests surrounding us. Not the okay I envisioned three months after our wedding when we saw *Cool Hand Luke*, and Luke, a convict played by Paul Newman, was eating fifty hard-boiled eggs to win a bet and avoid some harsh punishment, and Henry whispered in my ear, "I could eat fifty hard-boiled eggs!" But a sub-okay. The sub-okay of old people.

And so, in our somewhat new and unrecognizable combination, the two of us sat at the table, eating our eggs and toast.

# 21.

ixty-two-year-old Abigail is not just empathetic; she probably understands the feelings of others better than anyone I
know. Which makes her a caring friend and a gifted fiction
writer. She's also very funny. Abigail lives in Celo, a Quaker community in the North Carolina mountains. She's divorced from her
first husband, has a daughter who's about to be married. Her second
husband, whom she's been married to for twenty years, is seventy-
one, which probably makes her more aware of growing older than
most people her age.

"Oh, I think about aging all the time!" Abigail says. "I could keep
you on the phone for hours talking about it!"

Like others, she starts with the not-so-great. "There are a couple
of things I'm scared of. I'm scared of dementia . . . or any disability
that would mean someone else had to take care of me. This is an old
fear. Independence and intelligence were highly prized in my family,
and I've always been afraid of losing them. (*Flowers for Algernon* was
the most terrifying book I read when I was young!) Of course, there's
plenty of societal reinforcement for this fear . . . the way old people
are viewed, our emphasis on strength, competency, speed, etc. But
I also grew up thinking that if I was too needy, I wouldn't be loved."

She goes on, "That's the negative. But just this morning I was
lying in bed with Larry and I raised my arm and all of a sudden,

it looked exactly like my great-aunt's arm—my great-aunt on my French side. She was a passionate and brilliant history professor who survived both world wars. She's my model for old age. She wore sleeveless dresses, gesturing impatiently with her wrinkled, veiny, spotted arms as she chain-smoked unfiltered Gauloises and clacked her dentures in and out. My arms are just like hers now, and I love it! But because others will see the changes in my body as unattractive, I feel I should call attention to them in some way, make a joke, even apologize for them, so people will know that I know what is pretty and that I realize I've deviated from pretty. My great-aunt would never have worried about that!"

And then: "Beyond the fear of dementia and of not being loved and even thinking I don't look right, I'd a thousand times rather be this age than any other age. A thousand times."

And then: "I love that you're writing about aging, Judy. I've thought for years that we need the old person's version of *Our Bodies, Ourselves*."

———

My mother began developing signs of Alzheimer's in her early sixties. By sixty-five, her diminishment was so pronounced I wrote a poem about it. I was thirty-four. This was the first poem I read aloud to an audience, the first I ever revealed in any way to someone else. I had seen a notice about an open mic reading at Queens College, open to everyone, just show up, bring a poem. *I'll do it...I won't...I will...I can't.*

"Go, Judy!" Henry said. "You'll be glad you did." I'd left my job at Kincaid Advertising and had been working as a freelance ad copywriter for a number of years, as busy as I wanted to be because I was one of only two freelancers in Charlotte. But I was tired of selling architects and political candidates, savings accounts and natural gas. I was tired of writing to please committees. "I like this ad, Judy, but I showed it to my mother-in-law, and she thought it would sound better if you just . . ." I wanted to please only myself. I wanted to write poetry.

I went to the open reading. Read my poem. It was not a good poem. But reading it aloud, to a crowded room, marked the beginning of taking myself seriously as a writer. A gift Henry gave to me. A gift my mother's Alzheimer's gave to me.

---

When Mother was diagnosed, no one in our family had even heard of Alzheimer's. It was the mid-1970s. People still called what was happening to her *senility*. But she was not old enough to be senile. My doctor pulled out his heavy medical textbooks and allowed me to spend the afternoon at his desk in his private office reading about the disease.

My father did not believe the local neurologist who diagnosed Mother. "I'll just take her to Mayo Clinic," my father said. "We'll see what they have to say."

"Alzheimer's," the Mayo doctor said.

The last two years of Mother's life—she died from complications of Alzheimer's—were spent in a nursing home in Charlotte. She was unable to recognize anyone, to talk or walk. Alive and breathing, but that was about it. She had shrunk down to nothing. She moaned and writhed in the bed, even though Thorazine dampened her agitation. Guardrails held her in place. At one point, after my father had died and I was out of town and unreachable by phone, she must have indicated in some way—I can't imagine how—that she had a toothache. The nursing home transporter took her to the dentist, who removed all her teeth. Her face was no longer a valentine. It was sunken in. She looked like she was sucking her gums.

So many afternoons, I bundled her into a wheelchair, fastened the strap, and wheeled her down to the activities room to play the piano for her, hoping my music might reach her in a way my words couldn't. I had taken piano lessons growing up but didn't like the classical music my teacher assigned. I was ready to quit. Mother wanted me to stay with it. We reached a compromise. I'd take piano, but I could play any music I wanted.

I pulled Mother's wheelchair close to the piano bench and went through my repertoire. "Over the Rainbow"—surely, she'll remember that one. I used to play it every time I sat down at the piano. She just stared straight ahead. "Honeysuckle Rose." I began to play louder. "Sh-boom," "Me and My Shadow." Louder. Nothing. No response at all. I wasn't looking at the keys. I was searching her face. Not even a glimmer in those brown eyes.

It was a loss that grew deeper and deeper month after month. Such a prolonged loss. Her drawn-out illness, a limbo. She was not there. Yet she was there.

I never got used to pushing open the double front doors of the nursing home, never got used to taking the elevator all the way up—the higher the floor, the sicker the patient. Never got used to seeing her—*my mother*—parked beside the nurses' station, across from the elevator, that lineup of hazy women, wheels locked firmly in place, woolly robes, the stories of their lives no longer mattering.

If my bright, buoyant, engaged mother could lose her mind, anyone could. That's the thought that spiraled through my mind. There was no protection from life's horrors. I scrubbed my hands rough and red after every visit. As though I could wash away Alzheimer's bitter germs—and keep myself from being next.

My father had been diagnosed with colon cancer years before. Now his cancer had returned, colon cancer metastasizing into lung cancer metastasizing into bone cancer metastasizing into brain cancer. That's when he moved in with Brenda's family, then mine, so that he could be in Charlotte and spend his days at Mother's bedside. Gray-faced from his own illness, he would tell us each evening what a good day the two of them had had. That was my father. How many times, when Donald, Brenda, and I were growing up, did he say, "If you're going to do business, you have to do it in today's climate." We were not little businessmen. We were kids! What he meant was, you don't whine about the past, you don't whine about the present, you don't whine about how things should be. You accept.

I wrote poem after maudlin poem. A poet friend called me "the high priestess of loss." I was not doing business in today's climate. I believed that writing my endless stanzas about losing my parents would get me to another day.

I became hypervigilant. Henry called it my hospital personality. The minute I walked through the doors of the nursing home or a hospital or even a doctor's office, I became this other person. Assertive. No, aggressive. No, demanding. Checking behind every doctor and nurse, double-checking, second-guessing medications, tests, procedures, surgeries, whatever I had to do to keep my parents alive.

Still, everything kept spilling through my hands.

My father died first. January 1980.

Twenty months later, September 1981, Mother died.

The only good thing about losing both parents the way I did is that they were each spared the other's death. My father's death meant he did not have to endure losing Mother. And Mother was too far into the half sense of her mind to know when my father died.

Even when death is expected, it comes at you in unexpected ways. The death of my mother was, as you might imagine, a relief. I'd lived with loss for so long, but now I could mourn my loss. My mourning took on a shape I had not expected. Mother's clear and irrefutable death, after years of her deathlike existence, freed something in me, and I could finally picture her healthy and vibrant again. Memories of the past had been walled off to me, inaccessible. Now, they floated around my head like cologne.

Three weeks after Mother's death, I turned forty. I had heard her say many times that the forties were the best years of her life. The same way I'd looked forward to becoming a grandmother, I'd also looked forward to turning forty. (My fascination with the various stages of a life took many forms!) My mother's voice was the most important voice I heard while I was growing up. So, if she thought the forties were good, I was eager to see for myself. I was just a kid, a young thing reading *Motion Picture* magazine, tap dancing, imagining how great it would be to hit forty.

Turning forty *was* everything I'd expected it to be. My parents were no longer trapped in misery. It's not that I believed they were "in a better place," as people are quick to say. The best place for them, as far as I was concerned, was to still be alive and healthy. But I was relieved to no longer be fighting to *keep* them alive. My children were growing up. I was writing poetry more and more, freelancing ad copy less and less. The rest of my life was beginning.

———

Now, the hypervigilance of those years is back. Maybe it never went away. Henry has had cancer of a minor salivary gland, a stroke, kidney stones, hernias, gout, back surgeries, joint replacements, reactions to meds and to anesthesia, middle-of-the-night runs to the ER, blood clots, serious medical mishaps, complications. I've been lucky in that all I've had is breast cancer. That was many years ago but still, it seems we're all hovering on the edge between fine and not-fine. Which, in my wild imagination, convinces me the little things that crop up are more than little things. This red place on my cheek, I'm sure, is something terrible. Henry's blood pressure up? Uh-oh. I pay close attention, Google red places on cheeks and blood pressure, ask the doctor a million questions.

Bad things can happen. But I'm going to prevent them. I tighten my grip.

Still, the world keeps passing away.

Nothing is constant.

Eternal youth? Immortality? We won't attain either.

My granddaughter Zoe, when she was eight, asked me, "Gaygay, were you around during the Civil War?"

To a young person, old is old. To an old person, old is loss.

Because what is life other than dealing with variations of loss? Loss of childhood, loss of innocence, loss of opportunity, loss of dreams, loss of stature, loss of purpose, loss of identity, loss of time, loss of energy, loss of balance, loss of attractiveness, loss of protection, loss of love.

I'm really okay with dying. Even talk of death doesn't scare me. I'm just not that crazy about loss.

We're all trying to discover a way to go on, in spite of the inevitability—and the irreversibility—of loss. How do we learn to live with the knowledge that this person whom we love so much, we will lose? The knowledge is especially biting if we're talking about a mate. He will die. Or I will die.

Our friend Lew's thought: *But there's no denying that one of us will come to sleep alone in our double bed . . .*

My thought: *One of us will wake up in the morning, flip the pillow to the cool underside, roll over, alone, all alone, no one on the other side of our queen-size bed to ask, "How'd you sleep?"*

# 22.

For as long as I could remember, my mother wore a loose, yellow- and pink-gold bracelet of tiny, scalloped shells. One day—she understood she had Alzheimer's, but she was still living at home and managing well enough—we were sitting together on the sofa in her living room. My memory is that it was a winter afternoon. If we had looked out the window, we would've seen bare black branches framing the thirteenth fairway. She said, in her halting speech—Alzheimer's was taking what it could, when it could—that she had a present for me.

"I want you . . . um . . . to have . . . um . . . this . . ." As though she needed a map to say a single sentence. Still, I sensed something of importance about to happen.

And it did turn out to be just that. She slid the bracelet off her rosy wrist and held it out, a cluster of shimmery shells in her palm. I took the bracelet, slid it over my hand, and held it up for us to admire.

"This . . . um . . . makes me . . . um . . . so . . . happy!" she said, patting my arm. She had given me everything. And now, this.

I wore that bracelet through the worst days of her illness, through her death, and for years after.

One weekend Henry and I were in Wrightsville Beach. Late afternoon, we left the shade of our umbrella by the ocean to go shopping at Reddix, our favorite store in Wrightsville, one we'd shopped in many times over the years. In one large room, there were dozens of circular racks—too many to count—holding women's clothes. I was making my way around, pulling out shorts and tops and bathing suits to try on. Henry was in the men's section, trying on wide-brimmed sun hats, which he always does when we go to a beach shop. Every now and then, he comes to find me to show how a particular hat looks. He never actually buys one.

That night, back in our hotel, we were getting ready for bed. I started to take off my bracelet. But there was no bracelet. Gone. Vanished from my arm. I could hardly absorb the sight of my bare wrist. *It's got to be in the store. We'll find it. For sure, it'll be there.*

The next morning, before Reddix even opened, Henry and I were standing at the front door, our faces pressed to the glass.

As soon as they let us in, we combed the floor beneath the racks, lifting the clothes so we could see all the way across. We searched the dressing room I'd used, the sun hat department, the area around the cash register, the route from the cash register to the front door to the parking lot. No bracelet. Back again. Now we were crawling beneath the bathing suits and shorts and tops—the rough, flat carpet. No luck.

One more day at the beach before we would leave for home. Still, the hope that someone from the store would call my cell phone, tell me my bracelet had been found, they'd leave it up front at the cash register with my name, they were so happy to give me this good news.

The afternoon we drove away from Wrightsville Beach, I knew I would never see my bracelet again.

During our ride home, Laurie called from Durham to say that the age for having a mammogram had been lowered to thirty-five, so she'd gone in for hers. Her mammogram had revealed a mass in her breast, and she was scheduled for a biopsy the next morning. A shock. And a scare. She was so young, her twins only three years old. I wished she had told us about the mass when they'd first discovered it.

"Do you want me to come to Durham, to be with you when you have your biopsy?"

"No, no," she said. "It's okay. I'll let y'all know as soon as I hear."

I decided that moment: *Okay. I'll give up my bracelet. Just let Laurie's mass be benign. I'll gladly give up one for the other.*

And it *was* benign. And my loss became a gain.

———

Anyway, I still have the thin, ropy gold heart pin our father asked Brenda to go to Tiffany's to buy—one for her, one for me, one for Donald's wife, Mara. Brenda had taken our father to Sloan Kettering in New York City for a second opinion after his cancer had returned. Years before, he'd had colon surgery, then lung surgery. That's when the doctor at Sloan Kettering said the wrong surgery had been performed that second time. It should have been on the colon again, not the lung. There was nothing the doctor could do. My father did not have long to live.

Minutes after our father heard the news, he told Brenda to take his wallet, go to Tiffany's, and buy something special, something meaningful, the same gift for all three of his "daughters."

I'd stayed behind to look after Mother, who was still at home but fading rapidly. Back and forth from Charlotte to Rock Hill I went. Then, a snowstorm, and no caregiver could get to her house, so I spent two nights taking care of her. I cooked, played the piano for her, took her into the shower with me. But when the roads cleared and I heard my father's diagnosis, I *had* to go to New York City. I couldn't spend another day not seeing him. I knew he had months, but it felt like they'd said hours.

I wear my heart pin often. It brings back my father's hospital room, the view of the New York City street from his window, the escalator we took from the lobby up to his room, his bravery facing the news, his good humor, the snowy evening we took him out—against hospital rules—and we (our father, Brenda, Donald, and I) had dinner in a cozy, lantern-lit restaurant. It felt like the flames in those polished brass lanterns high on the walls were warming us.

My heart pin brings back my father's determination to leave a token of his affection. The idea that he instructed Brenda to go to Tiffany's, of all places. So out of character for him. He was always very careful with money. Never in favor of buying anything extravagant. And, more important, he had not been the most openly affectionate father in the world while we were growing up. You would describe him as loving, but no-nonsense, down-to-business. As Mother was disappearing, though, he *became* her. Sentimental, sensitive, openly affectionate. Which is why the heart pin was so significant.

Maybe he knew, maybe Mother knew, that when we lose the people we love, we become even more attached to the possessions we own that bring them back.

———

This story has a sad P.S. A few years after our father died, Brenda lost her heart pin. Mara, divorced from Donald but still close to Brenda and me, gave her pin to Brenda. A generous and touching gesture. But then, Brenda lost *that* pin.

We have to learn, over and over, that something which was just here can be, all of a sudden, gone.

# 23.

I catch John S. (Trisha's husband), eighty-one, sitting on a log out in the woods on a fifty-five-degree January afternoon, his dog, Molly, scratching up the leaves. John is retired from the computer rental business he owned. He volunteers at Crisis Assistance Ministry and spends part of every day riding his horse, Bo. When I ask for his thoughts on growing old, at first he wants to take some time thinking about the subject and call me later. But I say that I'd really like his spontaneous thoughts. Always genial, always good-natured, always willing to explore weighty questions like this, he jumps right in.

"Here's Thought Number One: The great thing about being in your eighties, you no longer have to pretend to be somebody you think you should be. You can discover and be, in fact, who you really are. Part of it is discovery. And even some experimentation. That would be my biggest, biggest takeaway."

"And Thought Number Two?" I ask.

"Did I say I had more thoughts?"

"You started with Thought Number One."

"Oh. Well, that's my only thought."

———

I call Bill, brainy, verbally dexterous (you can see semicolons when he talks), soon to be eighty-four, who tells me he's almost out the door to play tennis. His wife, Clarissa, a member of the original Breakfast Group, died in 2012. He and Clarissa had each been married before. Bill is now married to Peggy, who reminds me so much of Clarissa I might have thought to introduce them had I known Peggy. Bill is a retired hematologist and oncologist and—his own words—retired thanatologist. His last years of work were with hospice, "helping people to die comfortably."

His thoughts:

"The good news is that I've got my tennis togs on. I'm still able to play tennis. The bad news is that I can't get to the balls I used to get to."

I mention Laurie J.'s commentary on aging, how she wishes she still *wanted* to do things. "But you're still passionate about things, it sounds like."

"Well," he says, "I'm wistful about romance and the physical expressions thereof. If I take a pill, maybe I can perform. If I don't take a pill, I won't perform. I wish I cared more, but that's another problem that goes with aging ... the inability to have sex and the inability to care whether you do or not. Peggy and I start each day reading poetry together. We end each day reading a novel aloud to each other. This morning, we were reading "Singapore" by Mary Oliver. I have never been to Singapore. But I don't want to go. I think that comes with age ... or it comes with wherever I am on my journey. Big picture ... I know what's coming. I know what's been. I'm grateful I'm able to do the things I do. I'm part of a demographic that won't be around much longer. I don't spend a lot of time fretting about that. I'm just aware of it."

The next morning Bill emails additional thoughts:

I read several years ago that one should think about one's death every day, and I certainly do, though the mystery of what happens after I'm gone (nothing, I guess) endures. I just know that death gets closer every day, and the world will little note nor long remember that I was once part of it. I'm reminded of the Willa Cather story of a horse-drawn sled being pursued one snowy night by wolves. The occupants keep throwing things out of the sled in order to escape, but the wolves are not deterred and ultimately catch up and have their way.

For us creatures who concern ourselves with trying to get ready for what's next, for us creatures privileged enough to have the good health and luxury of time and resources to reflect, there are questions. You'd think we'd be asking the big, important questions about living and dying. But instead, we ask:

If I chew on this ice, will I break a tooth?

Will Lucy, Zoe, Tess, and Benjamin remember me?

If Henry has another stroke, will Laurie and Mike be in town? What if they're both away?

Is that blood I see seeping through Henry's compression sock on his bad leg?

I'm taking mac and cheese, sweet potato casserole, and brownies to Mike and Brooke's for Thanksgiving. How will I get all that down to the garage and into our car?

What are these funny lumpy things appearing on my forehead?

I don't need to send out holiday cards anymore, do I?

If we never use that oily cleanser on the refrigerator door again, which means not a single slippery drop on the floor, does that mean I won't ever have another fall?

If we stay in the condo, will medics figure out how to get into the building and up to the fourth floor?

Near the end of life—after experiencing loss, in the midst of loss, anticipating loss up ahead, right there—these are the questions that want answering most of all. It's the ordinary part of us taking over, balancing out what might be missing and what will be found.

It's us, getting comfortable with the tension.

Learning to experience this ever-shifting world as it truly is.

Honoring, not fighting, reality.

Doing business in today's climate.

Figuring out what life is supposed to be about, what counts.

Living with a handful of years left.

Reducing what it takes to make us content.

Landing on curiosity instead of fear or worry.

Understanding that it all funnels down to wonderment in the day after day.

Being attentive, being patient, lingering in thought.

Coming to terms with the fact that we can't really know what the best course of action is.

Dishing up hope. Things carrying on.

# 24.

"I'm done. I will never write another book."

That was me, not so long ago. Normally, when I've finished a book and it's about to be published, I have an idea for a new book. But my last memoir was moving toward publication, and I did not think I had another book in me. What was left to write about?

I'd started writing poetry in 1949, when I was eight. My first poem was titled "My Friend, Joe." I not only didn't have a friend named Joe; I'd never even known anyone named Joe. I picked the name because so many words rhymed with it. *Ago, Moe, hoe* were three I came up with. That same year I began keeping a diary, filling every page from January 1 to December 31, locking the diary tight with the little key, hiding the key from my sister in a sock in my underwear drawer. I wrote in diaries every year until I graduated from high school. Also, during my early years, I made little illustrated books about my future: "My Life as a Movie Star," "My Life as a Tap Dancer," "My Life as a Teacher." I wrote, and Brenda illustrated, a neighborhood newspaper that we sold up and down our street.

In my twenties, a young wife and mother, I wrote in journals.

In my thirties, when both my parents were sick and dying, I found my way back to poetry. I was so sad, I could easily have taken to my bed. I took to my typewriter instead.

I stayed with poetry through my forties. But then the lines in my poems started stretching from margin to margin. I tried to beat them into submission. You *will* be a poem! Finally, I realized those weren't stanzas; they were paragraphs. I was yearning to write prose.

I knew I had only just begun to catch on to what writing poetry was all about. *Do I just switch to prose? Surely, that's not a smart strategy, hopping to a new genre before I master the old one. And . . . how to switch?*

I was fifty-three when Henry and I flew to Maine, staying in bed and breakfasts across the state. On the front table in a used bookstore in Blue Hill, I spotted the novel *Monkeys* by Susan Minot. Henry was elsewhere in the store, probably looking for a book he'd heard about on NPR. I remembered reading a review of *Monkeys* when it had been published years earlier.

The rest of our trip, I read that book, *studied* that book—in our rental car, as Henry navigated back roads, unfolding the AAA map with one hand and steering with the other; in lobster shacks by the side of the road; in high canopy beds under heavy quilts before flicking off a rickety lamp.

Then I read it again, making about a million notes in the margins. I believe I wrote more words in that book than the author did.

Here's a sentence from *Monkeys*:

"On Sunday nights we have treats and BLTs and get to watch Ted Mack and Ed Sullivan."

———

You can write a whole book just about family? So many scenes in *Monkeys* brought back scenes from my childhood. The family in Minot's autobiographical novel was upper-class, Catholic, New England.

Seven children. My family was middle-class, Jewish, Southern. It was just Donald, Brenda, and me.

Susan Minot's family and my family had nothing in common.

But the message I got from her novel: *You can do this, Judy.*

I believe most writers can name the book that told them they could write. That trigger to begin. *Monkeys* told me I could write prose. Prose that centered on my family, myself. When Henry and I returned home from Maine, I began writing my first novel.

Which led, a few years later, to a second novel.

Then, on to something even more personal: a memoir. And a second memoir.

And, in my late seventies, a third memoir.

After the publication date for that last memoir had been set, when I would normally begin thinking about writing something new, I did not see how I would ever be able to do it again. I kept clearing my throat, but no words came.

I was far from happy over the prospect of giving up writing. How would I fill my days? Occupy my mind? Writing is what keeps me nice. If I'm not writing, I'm not a person you want to be around. Writing also keeps me from overworrying about my husband, children, grandchildren, self.

———

During a Zoom call with Abigail, Darnell, and John, fellow writers, I told them I was done. That was it. No more writing. But just in case I ever decided to go back to it, would they tell me how they get started, what they do when they have the motivation to write, but no idea?

"Buy a notebook and jot down anything that pops in your head," they all said.

Of course! I knew this approach. It was how I'd started every book I'd ever written. But would that work this time?

I pulled a little brown notebook from the bottom drawer of my rolltop desk. It was thin, very thin, because I believed very few ideas, if any, would come.

Days passed. The notebook sat on the edge of my desk, blank. If it's possible for an inanimate object to crook a forefinger to try to coax you over, that thing did.

Finally, on the first page, I wrote:

*something about aging*

A week, maybe two weeks later, I made these notes on the first page, right below *something about aging*:

*something about life passages—Atlanta, NYC, marriage, looks*

More notes in my thin little brown notebook:

*We all have a birth story—my house has a birth story—a genesis story —Uncle Irwin—house not well constructed. Compare to housing now?*

*Grandparents... none for me, none for Laurie and Mike*

*NYC = new territory*

Would all these notes amount to anything? Do we ever know if what we write will amount to anything?

Do we ever know if what we try to do *in any area of our life* will amount to anything?

The problem of doubt.

Really, here's what was keeping me from typing *Chapter One* on a blank page in my computer—the thought that I was just too old to write another book.

But then another thought broke through: Maybe that's why I *should* write. *Because* I'm old. If the various stages in my life have provided me with subject matter—I live it, then relive it on the page—why would I stop writing before I take on this final stage?

The book you're holding in your hands is all about doubt. Not just doubt in writing, of course. Mostly *not* in writing. This book asks how, despite doubt, we can move through this one tiny moment and the next tiny moment. Through the weather. Through change.

Lordy (the word my mother used on almost every page of her 1929 diary), we have no idea what we're doing. We are *not ready.* Still, we must defy that ghosty person sitting on our shoulder, the one who keeps whispering, "You can't do this." We have to trust that good outcomes can exist on the other side of unsureness.

Just by living, proceeding through time, minutes and hours, we learn, bit by bit, the truth of who we are. Everything we experience, how we react to what we experience, the decisions we make by deciding or not deciding, the thing done or not done, this time like that time—the back-and-forthing—all of it reveals who we are. All of it amounts to a life.

In writing, we proceed through the pages, which is how we learn, bit by bit, what our story is about. It's not fully visible in the beginning. The writer rummages through the possibilities, fixes on life at its smallest, the ordinary details, and . . . something gets written.

If we're lucky enough to see our words end up in books, we hope our books will survive across time in a way that our bodies can't. We hope some day our books will be the possessions we've left behind. Maybe they'll occupy a space on the shelves in our grandchildren's homes. Maybe our loved ones will be attached to our books because they bring us back.

*Will Lucy, Zoe, Tess, and Benjamin remember me?*

Do I have enough years left to finish this book? Will I still be working on it after I move into assisted living at Sharon Towers? Are computers even allowed in assisted living?

Judy. Stop. You have the rest of your life to do this.

You have the rest of your life.

# Author's Note

I changed some people's names to protect their privacy.

Also, I've tried to be as accurate as possible with details, but if there are any mistakes in these pages, I'm the one you blame.

One more thing: I wrote this book when I was eighty. And then I revised. And grew older. I did not update details in the narrative. I decided to keep it a snapshot in time.

# Acknowledgments

I love writing acknowledgments! It gives me the opportunity to think of all the people who got me here. Even though I'm the one who, for years, sat in this not-very-comfortable but attractive Ikea desk chair, fingers tapping the keyboard, trying to turn these sentences into something that might matter, I couldn't have done it without the family and friends and book people who surround me.

#1, Henry. For close to sixty years, he and I have argued over which of us is the lucky one. He's just being polite when he says he is. I'm totally honest when I say it's me.

Laurie and Bob, Mike and Brooke. I was smart to bring Laurie and Mike into the world, and they were smart to bring Bob and Brooke into our family.

Special gratitude to Laurie for this gorgeous book cover (which uses a portal painting of hers), hours of tech help, and my fabulous website (judygoldman.com).

In loving memory of my parents, Peggy and Ben Kurtz; my brother, Donald; my sister, Brenda; and Mattie.

And the rest of my family, dear people: my cousin Debbie; adopted sister, Mara; nephews and nieces—Jeff and Sherry; Doug and Ashli; Adam and Cooper; 'Leen; Tina; Brian and Tonya; Scott and Lisa; Danny and Diana; Sasha and Dave; Tracy. In loving memory of nephews David and Steven.

My much-loved breakfast group: Bobbie, Laurie J., Trisha, (and Ann). In loving memory of Dannye, Mary Hunter, and Clarissa.

Old friends, good friends: Abigail, Judy, Mary, Marilyn, Paula, Kathryne, Betsy, Nancy Jan, Marilee, Darnell, Georgann, Donna, Kristen and Bob, Alice, Chris, Beth.

Friends who were willing to be interviewed for this book: Dannye, Trisha, Laurie J., Bobbie, Judy, Nancy Jan, Betsy, Darnell, Marilee, Kathryne, Marilyn, Lew, John J., Abigail, John S., Bill. How clever of me to know such perceptive people!

Bookstore friends across the Carolinas, especially Sally and Halli at hometown Park Road Books, who look after me, book after book. Charlotte Lit friends Kathie, Paul, and Paula, who look after me, book after book.

Star readers—Abigail, Darnell, Maya, Paul. My first readers—Henry, Laurie, and Mike. Thank you all for catching the places I go astray.

My agent, Grainne. Smart and tall and beautiful and the biggest heart in the world.

My publisher, Lynn. I've known you for so long and now I get to work with you, and it is just as full of pleasure as I knew it would be. Thank you for your keen eye, your good brain, your kind self. Robin, Arielle, Michael, and Jessica—my new publishing friends—thank y'all for the amazing work you do.